PLAY IN EARLY CHILDHOOD

Based on the pioneering work of Mary D. Sheridan, *Play in Early Childhood* is a classic introductory text to play and development – key topics for all those who work with young children. Updated for a contemporary audience and fully evidence-based, it explains how children's play develops and how they develop as they play.

With over eighty illustrations and observations of play from birth to six years, this new edition presents classical and contemporary literature, making clear links between play and all areas of children's development. It includes activities to consolidate thinking and suggestions for further reading throughout. *Play in Early Childhood* considers:

- the development, value and characteristics of play;
- issues relating to culture, adversity and gender;
- play from recreational, therapeutic and educational perspectives;
- the role of parents/caregivers and professionals in supporting play.

Suitable for those new to the area or for more experienced workers wanting a quick reference guide, this easy-to-follow book meets the needs of students and professionals from a wide range of health, education and social care backgrounds, including early years professionals, playworkers, children's nurses, speech and language therapists and social workers.

Mary D. Sheridan was a renowned researcher in child development and the author of *From Birth to Five Years* (Routledge, 2007).

Justine Howard is a chartered psychologist and developmental and therapeutic play specialist. She is a senior lecturer at Swansea University where she is responsible for a number of courses relating to play and child development.

Dawn Alderson is a senior academic tutor in the School of Human and Health Science at Swansea University where she teaches on postgraduate courses relating to play and creativity.

PLAY IN EARLY CHILDHOOD

From birth to six years

3rd edition

Mary D. Sheridan

Revised and updated by
Justine Howard and Dawn Alderson

 Routledge
Taylor & Francis Group

LONDON AND NEW YORK

KH

First published 2011
by Routledge
2 Park Square, Milton Park, Abingdon, Oxon, OX14 4RN

Simultaneously published in the USA and Canada
by Routledge
270 Madison Avenue, New York, NY 10016

Routledge is an imprint of the Taylor & Francis Group, an informa business

© 1977, 2011 Mary D. Sheridan. Revised and updated by Justine Howard and
Dawn Alderson

The right of Mary D. Sheridan, Justine Howard and Dawn Alderson to be
identified as authors of this work has been asserted by them in accordance with
sections 77 and 78 of the Copyright, Designs and Patents Act 1988.

Typeset in Sabon
by Keystroke, Station Road, Codsall, Wolverhampton
Printed and bound in Great Britain
by MPG Books Group, UK

British Library Cataloguing in Publication Data
A catalogue record for this book is available from the British Library

Library of Congress Cataloging in Publication Data
Play in early childhood : from birth to six years /
Mary D. Sheridan. – 3rd ed., rev. and updated / by Justine Howard
and Dawn Alderson.
p. ; cm.
Includes bibliographical references.
1. Play. I. Howard, Justine. II. Alderson, Dawn. III. Title.
[DNLM: 1. Play and Playthings. 2. Child Development. 3. Child, Preschool.
4. Infant. WS 105.5.P5]
HQ782.S53 2011
155.4'18–dc22
2010030194

ISBN13: 978–0–415–57789–2 (hbk)
ISBN13: 978–0–415–57790–8 (pbk)
ISBN13: 978–0–203–83260–8 (ebk)

9/2/11

Contents

About the authors

Mary D. Sheridan was a highly respected community paediatrician and health educator, with more than forty years of experience in supporting children's health and development. Her pioneering work, including the extensive documentation of children's development, led to the production of two influential and well-received texts, *Children's Developmental Progress* (1975) and *Spontaneous Play in Early Childhood* (1977). The timeless value of her work is evident in the continued popularity of revised versions of these texts, which, based on observations of real children in real situations, continue to support parents and professionals working in a variety of contexts.

Justine Howard is a chartered psychologist and developmental and therapeutic play specialist. She has wide-ranging classroom experience and has worked for a number of years alongside children with additional learning needs, before training in psychology and, later, in therapeutic play. She specializes in developmental psychology and the psychology of education. Her Ph.D. focused on children's perceptions of their play and she has since spent more than a decade researching this area. She is particularly interested in how play contributes to children's development and wellbeing and her work has resulted in numerous publications. Justine is the programme director of the MA in Developmental and Therapeutic Play at Swansea University.

Dawn Alderson has a background in primary teaching and has been a senior academic tutor at Swansea University since 2002. She has been involved with initial and in-service teacher training and currently lectures on undergraduate and postgraduate courses in the School of Human and Health Science. She has a master's degree in education which focused on meta-cognition in the early years. More recently Dawn has been involved with research and freelance work in the areas of play, children's health and wellbeing and creativity in education. She is in the latter stages of completing a doctorate in education about creative partnerships with upper-primary-aged children in Wales.

Introduction

In his foreword to the original version of this book – Mary Sheridan's *Spontaneous Play in Early Childhood* (1977) – Professor Jack Tizard described how at the time of Sheridan's writing, services concerned with children's intellectual, physical and social needs were grounded in knowledge about the nature of child development. Sheridan's observations of children's spontaneous play were invaluable in providing practitioners with an insight into the development of 'real children in real situations', allowing the reader to enrich their theoretical knowledge and validate their own experiences.

Play is recognized in Article 31 of the United Nations Convention on the Rights of the Child (United Nations, 1989) and a growing evidence base as to the value of play for children's development, health and wellbeing has contributed to governmental policies designed to ensure that all children have access to appropriate play experiences. There are initiatives promoting recreational play opportunities, sport and leisure activities, and play is pivotal within school curricula designed for children in the early years. There could not be a more appropriate time for us to return to a basic consideration of how children's play develops and how they develop as they play.

We would all agree that understanding children's development remains at the heart of services for children. However, publications for practitioners are often now directed towards the area in which we work: for example, separate publications are written for teachers, nurses and other play specialists. As we describe in Chapter 5, this often means that children's development is discussed within a particular context or with a particular developmental outcome in mind. In educational texts, for example, there might be a much more substantial focus on learning through play rather than on children's growing ability to play. However, *learning through play* relies on children's *ability to play*; and understanding this, by reference to theories of child development and detailed observations and illustrations (such as those of Sheridan), remains invaluable. A teacher who observes a child who does not engage in role play, for example, becomes able to ask themself why this might be the case. Does the child have the skills necessary for this type of play? Should my next step be to try to encourage them to engage in role play or should I provide different play opportunities that might help in the development of their representational abilities? Similarly, how might a child with mobility, sensory or co-ordination difficulties be encouraged to learn more about the properties of objects to enrich their play? Using knowledge of how children's play usually develops and the skills associated with this was precisely what motivated Sheridan to write this book, so that she could provide the highest level of support for the children in her care.

Much has been written about play, and within an introductory text of this kind it is impossible to offer comprehensive coverage of all issues. Similarly, the depth to which issues might be discussed is also limited. Rather than oversimplifying the complexities that surround, for example, the play of children who are deaf or physically disabled or facing adversity, we have attempted to indicate the kinds of challenges these children might face and the kinds of questions we might ask in order to understand and best support their play. Sheridan's focus was on spontaneity in play, and a theme that emerges throughout this book is that children's spontaneous play is defined by a sense of freedom, choice and control. These features unify play professionals working across a variety of contexts and ensure inclusive practice. A sense of freedom, choice and control in play means that boundaries are set and regulated by children themselves. As a result, play promotes and protects esteem and maintains attention so that learning can take place.

As Professor Tizard noted, Sheridan's original work was undistorted by theory but her knowledge of child development is clearly evident through her observations. As her book on play was an accompaniment to her more substantial book on children's development, perhaps explicit reference to theory was not considered necessary. In addition, Sheridan was keen for her work not to become overly laden with scientific and controlled laboratory-type studies, which she believed detracted from the value of her first-hand observations. We have endeavoured to enhance Sheridan's original work with the careful introduction of supporting literature, including some key theoretical ideas and selected research. We hope that providing this context will ensure that readers gain maximum benefit from the depth and detail of her observations. We have tried to maintain a focus on children's growing repertoire of play skills while at the same time considering the developmental potential of play from social, emotional, linguistic, physical and intellectual perspectives. In addition, we have tried to offer scope for readers to develop their own philosophy of play through reflective activities and further reading.

Professor Tizard acknowledged the special place of Mary Sheridan in British paediatrics, noting her as the most distinguished and senior practitioner in the field. We hope that this revised edition serves to ensure that readers continue to benefit from her experience and expertise. It is a great privilege to have been asked to revise her work.

Justine Howard
Dawn Alderson

1   Theorizing about play

Consistent with the original Sheridan text, this chapter will focus on definitions of play, functions of play and predominant play types.

The specific aims of the chapter are:

■ To consider the issue of defining play and, in doing so, to highlight play as a *behaviour*, a *process* and an *approach to task*.

■ To consider why children play and what makes it valuable from a developmental perspective.

■ To introduce play types in which children typically engage and play types through which children typically progress.

■ To highlight that play both influences and reflects children's development.

Defining play

When we begin to study any given concept or phenomenon, one of the first steps we take is to define what we understand that concept or phenomenon to mean. What is play and how is it different from other types of behaviour? While everyone has some idea about what it means to play and what play might look like, deciding on a clear and agreed definition has proven problematic. Indeed, it has been argued that play is so complex that it defies definition (Moyles, 1989). Considering the struggle to define play, however, provides an important narrative that reveals the complexity of play as a behaviour, a process and an approach to task. In particular, the freedom and choice inherent in spontaneous play make it a vital ingredient for children's healthy development.

Sheridan (1977) writes:

For the purpose of my own deliberations and discussions I evolved the following:

- *Play* is the eager engagement in pleasurable physical or mental effort to obtain emotional satisfaction.

- *Work* is the voluntary engagement in disciplined physical or mental effort to obtain material benefit.

- *Drudgery* is the enforced engagement in distasteful physical or mental effort to obtain the means of survival.

- We all know that play and work may merge into each other (I would define this as *ploy*), and work and drudgery may also merge (I would define this as *slog*), but play and drudgery are incompatible.

- The everyday world of school children provides a foretaste of the adult world in that their daily work consists of uneven and fluctuating combinations of ploy, acquired competence and slog, just as our own work consists of varying amounts of exciting research, skilled practices, and pedestrian plodding.

Dictionary definitions of play suggest it is characterized by being frivolous, fun or light-hearted. However, this is at odds with the deep seriousness that can often be apparent when we observe children at play. Some theorists have suggested that for an activity to be regarded as play, certain characteristics must be observed. For example, Krasnor and Pepler (1980) suggest that for an activity to be defined as play, we must observe voluntary participation, enjoyment, intrinsic motivation, pretence and a focus on process over product. A problem with this type of approach, however, is that while these characteristics might be clearly evident in some instances of play, in other situations they are more difficult, if not impossible, to identify. Pellegrini (1991) proposes that the more characteristics

Play as a behaviour

that are present, the more like play the activity becomes. However, what if some of these characteristics are more important to play than others? Or what if two different observers see things differently? For example, one observer might believe that an activity being voluntary is far more important than it not having an end product, whereas another observer might make their decision based on signs of fun and enjoyment. Let's consider two examples of children playing with Lego blocks.

- Child (A) takes the blocks from the toy shelf in their bedroom. They take them to the table and become intently focused on building a replica of the model presented on the box packaging. There is no laughter or smiling; they appear lost in concentration, searching for the pieces and frequently glancing towards the box, checking if their structure is the same as the one pictured.

- Child (B) is handed the Lego blocks by their teacher and they take them to the carpet. They appear to be haphazardly building the bricks, the structure takes no particular form, and they change what they do as they go along. Sometimes they organize the bricks into piles by colour. Sometimes they put the bricks in piles according to size. They occasionally smile and laugh as they build up the bricks and then knock them down.

Which of these activities would be defined as play? Child (A) chose to take part in the activity, there is clearly an end product and there are no overt signs of pleasure and enjoyment. The activity was chosen for Child (B), they showed signs that the activity was enjoyable and fun and they didn't appear to be working towards any end product or goal. Neither of the scenarios demonstrates any element of pretence.

In fact, both of the children described their activities as play and this highlights how seeing play from an observational perspective can be problematic. Our approach to defining play is often based on adult views of what play looks like, rather than taking the child's perspective, and play means different things to different people at different times (Howard, 2009). For example, the 'play' of the professional footballer will be very different from the 'play' that occurs between friends at an after-school knock-around (Saracho, 1990). It seems that to understand play, we need to find out what players themselves think about the nature of their activities. Various types of play activity are detailed later in this chapter, but it is not enough for activities to look like play. We also need to understand what makes children approach activities in a playful way.

Play as an approach to task

Until quite recently, little research had focused on children's own perceptions of their play. Studies that have investigated what play means to children have been fruitful and have led to much deeper insight as to what separates play from other types of activity. Research demonstrates that preschool children define play as activity that is freely chosen and self-directed. Surprisingly, children do not often define play as being something that is necessarily fun (Robson, 1993; Keating *et al.*, 2000).

In addition to choice and control, activities that occur on the floor, rather than at a table, and outside, rather than inside, are more likely to be seen as play (Howard, 2002; Parker, 2007). The nature and degree of adult involvement are also important (McInnes *et al.*, 2009). Bundy (1993) argues that the way children approach an activity may be far more important than the actual activity itself. The same activity might be described by children as play or not play, depending on the freedom, choice and control they are afforded.

Play and exploration

The characteristics associated with play and non-play become particularly important when children enter a nursery or classroom situation and they begin to experience structured activities. It is here where we begin to see them comparing play with work activity in the way suggested by Sheridan. However, what about the play of babies and infants who have yet to make a distinction between play and other types of activity? Piaget (1951) and Hutt (1976) propose that activity progresses from exploration to play as children become familiar with objects and their environments. At the exploration stage, children are finding out what an object does; whereas during play, they begin to consider what they can do with that object. Therefore, much of the activity we can observe in young infants might be categorized as exploration. This exploration is comparable to the more structured learning experienced in later childhood. Early exploration is important as it acts as a springboard for the development of future play skills.

The dynamic process of play

Play is a behaviour, an approach to task, but also a process. Children move in and out of play according to their own needs and wishes and other influences within the environment. Other influences on children's play might include location, the availability of materials, time and the involvement of other people. Sturrock and Else (1998) suggest that play is a cycle of activity. They propose that children communicate the desire to play using a series of signals and that for play to maintain momentum these signals must be responded to appropriately. Perhaps the simplest example of this is one child inviting another to engage in a game of catch. Throwing a ball to another child might be seen as a signal or invitation to engage in the game. The second child responds to the signal and the ball is thrown back and forth. Then, one child decides they no longer wish to play the game and they stop returning the ball. The signal to play isn't responded to and the play comes to an end. Alternatively, the second child may decide they want to change the nature of the game and so they begin to bounce rather than throw the ball. They invite the original child to engage in a new game. If the original child bounces the ball back, they accept the game change and the flow continues. If not, they might either revert back to their original throwing behaviour in a bid to maintain the flow or end the play completely. In order to maintain a state of play, the needs and wishes of the players are negotiated. This process is similar to the flow state identified by Csikszentmihalyi and Csikszentmihalyi (1988), where choice and control over activity are said to lead to deep concentration, pleasure and satisfaction.

Functions of play

Sheridan's focus was on children's *spontaneous* play, suggesting a natural inclination or drive towards play activity. Early philosophical accounts explain spontaneous drive towards play as being the result of evolution or biological functioning:

■ *Pre-exercise theory* (Groos, 1901) suggests that play behaviour exists as a means of practising key skills that are essential to adult survival.

- *Recapitulation theory* (Hall, 1920) suggests that in play, children act out behaviours that were once essential for human survival but are no longer necessary, such as building dens or climbing trees.

- *Relaxation theory* (Patrick, 1916) suggests that we are driven to play because it involves minimal cognitive demands. Periods of play allow us to relax, storing energy in preparation for more important cognitive activity.

- *Surplus energy theory* (Spencer, 1898) suggests that play allows us to release excess energy that has not been spent fulfilling survival needs. As children are largely looked after by others, their unspent energy levels are high, resulting in the propensity to play.

Providing evidence as to why children seem to have a natural inclination towards play is difficult. It seems likely that there is a combination of reasons as to why play is children's preferred mode of action. Children certainly seem motivated to explore the world around them and to make sense of their experiences, and the development of their play skills seems to stem from this motivation. From their earliest sensory experiences and interactions with others, children develop a repertoire of play skills that support their development. Of importance is that children choose to learn about the world through play, and a sense of choice remains an important element of their play throughout childhood.

There is widespread recognition that children's play serves a useful developmental function. The role of play in promoting and supporting development has become a principal focus for scholars and professionals across many fields. We have seen the introduction of policies dedicated to ensuring that children have appropriate opportunities to play and the importance of play is recognized in Article 31 of the United Nations Convention on the Rights of the Child (United Nations, 1989). There is a history of play within children's services, and the specific role of play for learning, recreation and therapy is discussed further in Chapter 5.

Sheridan (1977) writes:

A child's developmental progress may be conveniently observed and defined within the context of the following parameters:

- *Motor Development* involving body postures and large movements. These combine high physical competence and economy of effort with precise forward planning in time and space.

- *Vision and Fine Movements* involving competence in seeing and looking (far and near) and manipulative skills, integrating sensory, motor, tactile and proprioceptive activities.

- *Hearing and Listening* and the *Use of Codes of Communication.*

- *Social Behaviour and Spontaneous Play* involving competence in organization of the self (i.e. self-identity, self-care and self-occupation), together with voluntary acceptance of cultural standards regarding personal behaviour and social demands.

Sheridan's recognition of the value of play in relation to the whole child, is echoed in recent documentation such as *Best Play* (Department for Culture, Media and Sport, 2000), which states that during play children learn and develop as individuals but also as members of the wider community.

- *Social and emotional development.* In play, children have the opportunity to learn about themselves and others. They become aware of the impact of their behaviour and develop skills in conflict resolution, negotiation, trust and acceptance. They can *try out* different ways of dealing with social situations and *try on* feelings, emotions and social roles.

- *Cognitive development.* Play offers opportunities to learn about objects, concepts and ideas: for example, sorting, sequencing, weight and balance. Children develop problem-solving strategies, and the ability to allow one thing to stand for something else (for example, in pretend play) is a precursor to more complex ways of thinking.

■ *Language development.* Play offers opportunities for the development of language skill in relation to vocabulary, pronunciation, sentence construction and the transmission of meaning and intent.

■ *Physical development.* Play involves gross and fine motor movements and as such promotes co-ordination and visuo-spatial ability. The increased aerobic activity resulting from sustained active play promotes physical health and fitness in terms of the cardio-vascular system, muscle tone and maintenance of optimum weight.

However, children learn in lots of different ways: for example, via imitation, by rote and through direct instruction. A key question for those studying play has been to identify what makes learning through play so valuable. Researchers have sought to be able to show that play, rather than other types of activity, makes a difference to children's development. With this in mind, we begin to appreciate the importance of clearly defining what play actually is.

Significant advances have been made here by focusing on children's perceptions of play. Research has shown that when children believe an activity to be play rather than work, their performance in problem-solving tasks is significantly improved and they show much deeper levels of engagement and motivation (McInnes *et al.*, 2009). Ring (2010) found that encouraging a playful approach to drawing in the early years by offering children freedom, choice and control led to increased participation and progress in their ability to use drawing as a tool for meaning making and communication. In addition, Whitebread (2010) demonstrated that during activities defined as play children show higher levels of meta-cognition and self-regulation.

These findings are consistent with the proposition that taking a playful approach to a task is far more important than the task itself (Bundy, 1993). While children learn in a number of different ways, their learning is enhanced across all developmental domains when an activity is approached as play. Sutton-Smith (1974) and Bruner (1979) suggest that playful activity is particularly beneficial for children's development as it promotes flexible thinking skills. Howard and Miles (2008) suggest that the improved performance evident when children approach tasks as play is a result of reduced behavioural thresholds. When children are in a playful mode, outcomes are flexible, fear is reduced and consequently more potential behaviours become available to try out. A sense of freedom, choice and control in play means that boundaries are set and regulated by children themselves. As a result, play promotes and protects esteem and maintains attention for learning to take place (Howard, 2010a).

Types of play

It is important to note that play both influences and reflects development. Some typologies of play document the activities we are likely to see children engaging in throughout the course of their childhoods. We can note how these different types of play are contributing to development. These typologies can be simplistic or complex.

Hutt (1976) proposes a distinction between *epistemic* play that focuses on the acquisition of knowledge and skill, and *ludic* play, which is more concerned with fantasy and make believe.

In contrast, Hughes (1999) has compiled an extensive typology that describes sixteen different play types:

- *Rough and tumble* – close-encounter activity involving touch, tickling and the use of relative strength with an indication that the activity is play
- *Socio-dramatic* – the enactment of real and potential human experience
- *Social* – play with rules for social engagement
- *Creative* – play that facilities a number of potential outcomes or responses
- *Communication* – play using words, nuances or gestures
- *Dramatic* – play which dramatizes events in which the child is not a direct participant

- *Symbolic* – play where one thing can stand for another

- *Deep* – play which allows the child to encounter risky experiences

- *Exploratory* – play to access factual information about objects or concepts

- *Fantasy* – play which rearranges the world in the child's way, a way which is unlikely to occur

- *Imaginative* – play where the conventional rules that govern the physical world do not apply

- *Locomotor* – movement in any or every direction for its own sake

- *Mastery* – control of the physical and affective ingredients of the environment

- *Object* – play which uses infinite and interesting sequences of hand–eye manipulations and movements

- *Role* – play exploring ways of being, although not normally of an intense personal, social, domestic or interpersonal nature

- *Recapitulative* – play that allows the child to explore ancestry, history, rituals, stories, rhymes, fire and darkness.

Other typologies of play have a more developmental focus and outline progression through certain play types as children acquire a growing repertoire of skills. Here the focus is on how children develop their ability to play.

Sheridan (1977) writes:

Different types of play emerge in developmental sequence as the child learns to use first their sensory and motor equipment to best advantage and later their powers of communication and creativity. Every step forward depends upon successful achievement of previous stepping-stones.

1 **Active play** presumes 'gross motor' control of head, trunk and limbs in sitting, crawling, standing, running, climbing, jumping, throwing, kicking, catching and so on. It is directly concerned with promotion of physical development and necessitates the provision of adequate free-ranging space to move about in, and natural obstacles to overcome, together with simple, safe, playground equipment, mobile and fixed.

2 **Exploratory and manipulative play**, beginning at about 3 months with finger play, presumes possession of age-appropriate gross-motor, fine-motor and sensory functioning. These components are essential not only for acquisition of hand–eye co-ordination, but also for attending to and localizing everyday sounds, for recognition of the permanence of objects and for learning to appreciate the implications of space and time. Integration of these separate physical and cognitive elements into total meaningful experience necessitates the availability of a number of simple things for manipulation, such as everyday domestic objects as well as traditional playthings like rattles, dolls, balls, building blocks, boxes, toys to grasp and move about by hand, and sound-making instruments.

3 **Imitative play** becomes clearly evident from 7–9 months. It presumes a child's ability to control their body, manipulate objects, integrate and interpret multi-sensorial experience and comprehend simple language, or perhaps, more accurately, their caregivers' vocal tunes. It reflects what a child sees and hears going on around them, providing a lively record of their perceptual learning. At first, this imitation is fragmentary and follows immediately upon the child's attention being attracted in some way to the activity which they imitate. Later they recall and repeat for their own amusement or for applause a series of these meaningful actions. Imitative play is necessary in order for a child not only to learn the quickest and most effective way of performing meaningful actions themselves, but also gradually

to understand that adults have differing roles and responsibilities.

4   **Constructive (or end-product) play**, beginning with very simple block-building at about 18–20 months, presumes possession of all the aforementioned motor and sensory abilities together with increasing capacity to make use of the intellectual processes involved in recognition and retrieval of previously stored memories. Additionally, it requires ability to create preliminary 'blueprints' in the mind and realize these in practical form. This type of play grows directly out of early exploratory and manipulative play, but also implies capacity to combine early 'pure' imitation with purposeful anticipation.

5   **Make-believe (or pretend) play**, beginning a couple of months before 2 years and elaborated for several years afterwards, presumes previous acquisition of all the foregoing types, particularly imitative role play. Having learned from experience the probable causes and effects relating to the activities they have observed and copied, children now deliberately invent increasingly complex make-believe situations for themselves, in order to practise and enjoy their acquired insights and skills. In this way they improve their general knowledge and, most importantly of all, refine their social communications. Make-believe play depends upon a child's ability to receive and express their ideas in some form of language-code. Consequently its spontaneous employment is of considerable diagnostic significance to professional workers concerned with the health, welfare and education of young children.

6   **Games-with-rules** presuppose a high degree of skill in all the foregoing types, including full understanding and acceptance of the abstractions involved in sharing, taking turns, fair play and accurate recording of results. They usually start at about 4 years when small groups of peer-

age children, under tacitly acknowledged leadership, improvise their own rules for co-operative play. Team games, which challenge competitiveness in older children and adults, become increasingly subject to rules imposed from without and, to be rewarding, must be played strictly according to the recognized constitution.

Sheridan observes how children's spontaneous play changes over time and the types of play she describes are consistent with theorists who suggest that play follows a developmental trajectory. It is generally accepted that the ages associated with any stage theory of development are approximate; however, of importance is the sequence in which behaviours emerge. The behaviours predominantly associated with one stage may occur concurrently with another and the play behaviours are cumulative, rather than exclusive. The progressive nature of play has been documented from a cognitive, social and emotional perspective.

Piaget (1951) proposed three stages of play that corresponded with cognitive development:

- *Practice play*: in the sensorimotor stage of development (approximately birth to two years), children explore their own bodies and the objects around them using sight, sound, touch and taste; the play here is often repetitive.

- *Symbolic play*: early in the pre-operational stage (approximately two to seven years), children develop the ability to allow one thing to stand for another and pretend play or make believe begins to emerge.

- *Games with rules*: in the latter part of the pre-operational stage of development and into the concrete operational stage (approximately age seven to eleven years) play becomes increasingly governed by rules.

Parten (1932) observed children aged two to five years in their preschool environment. Through extensive observations she noted that play became increasingly social with age. She described six social stages of play:

- *Unoccupied behaviour*: not playing, simply observing.

- *Solitary play*: child plays alone, uninterested in others.

- *Onlooker behaviour*: child watches the play of others and may talk to the children involved but this talk does not relate to the play.

- *Parallel play*: child plays alongside others, often imitating what is being played near by, but no interaction.

- *Associative play*: the children appear to be playing together but their activities are not organized.

- *Co-operative play*: playing together in more organized activities where they share intentions about the progress of the play.

Erikson (1963) focused on the emotional benefits of play and suggested that children's play served as a means of developing a sense of competence and positive self-esteem:

- *Autocosmic play*: during the first year of life, of most significance to Erikson was that early play focused on the child's exploration of the body and the senses. Awareness of the bodily self was seen as an important precursor to self-esteem in that we cannot evaluate the self without first having a basic awareness of what that self comprises.

- *Microspheric play*: in their second year, children begin to play with objects and during this time they begin to understand the impact that their own actions can have on the environment.

- *Macrospheric play*: at around three years, when children may enter preschool or nursery, play becomes more social. Activities are shared and children become aware that their environment and their sense of self are not only controlled by themselves but are influenced by others. They learn how to maintain a positive sense of self in the wider social world.

Summary

- Play reflects but also supports children's development.
- Play is more than just a behaviour; it is a process and a way of approaching an activity.
- Children are more likely to approach an activity as play when they are afforded freedom, choice and control.
- Development is enhanced when children approach activities as play.

Give yourself some time to think

Observe a child or group of children engaged in play.

- Why do you think the activity is play?
- Do you think the children would agree?
- In what ways do you think this play reflects and supports children's development?

Useful reading

Lester, S. and Russell, W. (2008) *Play for a Change*. London: National Children's Bureau, Central Books.

Smith, P. K. (2010) *Children and Play*. West Sussex: Wiley-Blackwell.

Observing the development of children's play 2

This chapter presents Sheridan's *original observations* of the ages and stages at which significant manifestations of behaviour usually appear, supporting the development of children's repertoire of play skills. Understanding children's development can help us to make the best provision for their play. However, it is important to bear in mind that wide variations are to be expected. The chapter describes children's development in age-defined sections; however, the ages provided should be taken only as a guide and they are not necessarily the earliest or latest points at which a behaviour might appear. This variation is evident in the illustrations used by Sheridan to exemplify her observations where sometimes, the age of the child pictured does not match the age with which the section is principally concerned. Of particular importance is the growth of children's ability to play and how their acquired play skills feed into further development. Note how Sheridan has captured the behaviours and skills she discusses within the illustrations.

The specific aims of this chapter are:

- To highlight the value of Sheridan's real-world observations in documenting children's development in play.

- To encourage readers, in light of the depth and detail presented by Sheridan, to reflect on their own observation skills.

Sheridan's observations 3-6 months

The newborn quickly learns to attract and welcome the attention of primary caregivers who are usually their first playmates. Although vigorous movements, smiles and coos indicate baby's response to enjoyable stimulation, behaviour becomes more purposeful over the coming months and is no longer merely a manifestation of stimulus and response but increasingly a question of selective sensory intake (reception) which is then processed within the brain (interpretation) and results in some appropriate motor outcome (expression).

6 weeks Caregivers are usually the first playmates and lively interchange involves looking, listening, vocalizing and body movements.

10 weeks Baby can grasp the bar and focus on a coloured ball, but is not yet able to co-ordinate hand and eyes.

12 weeks Lying on their front, they scratch at the table cover, enjoying simultaneous sight and sound.

3 months With head and back well supported baby demonstrates good hand–eye co-ordination in finger-play.

Hand–eye co-ordination is demonstrated at about 10–12 weeks when a recumbent child deliberately brings their hands together over the upper chest and engages in finger-play. About the same time, when lying on their stomach holding the head and shoulders up steadily, they will open and shut their hands to scratch the surface where they lie, with some appreciation of the simultaneous production of sight and sound. A handheld toy (such as a rattle) can be clasped and brought towards the face, but sometimes baby may bash their chin and any glances made at it are fleeting.

By about 14 weeks, baby develops increased control over head, neck and eye muscles simultaneously to hand grasp, and can hold the toy and steadily regard it. At about 18–20 weeks they can reach for and grasp an offered rattle, look at it with prolonged gaze and shake it. They can clasp and unclasp objects alternately and bring objects towards and away from the mouth.

By 6 months, muscular control, vision and hand–eye co-ordination are so advanced that baby can reach for and seize any nearby object. They have not yet developed voluntary hand release. They discover their feet and often use them as auxiliary claspers. Every grasped object is brought to the mouth. They are beginning to comprehend the permanence of people but not yet the permanence of things. When a toy falls from their hand, unless it is within their range of vision, it ceases to exist.

4½ months With consistent hand–eye co-ordination, baby holds the teething ring between their hands, opening and closing them alternately.

5½ months Baby discovers their feet and reaches out to them, demonstrating foot, hand and eye co-ordination.

6 months With high concentration, baby makes characteristic age-related two-handed approach to a block.

6 months A bell is grasped with both hands, the bell is transferred to one hand and then brought to the mouth.

Key observations

■ Develops a strong bond with responsive primary caregiver.

■ Hand–eye co-ordination improves and movements become more controlled and purposeful.

■ Objects are brought to the mouth for exploration.

■ Begins to understand the permanence of people but not objects.

6-12 months

At about 7 months baby is able to pass a toy from one hand to the other with voluntary hand release. From about 8 months, baby can sit steadily on the floor, stretch out in all directions for toys within reach without falling over, and is able to reach towards eye-catching objects.

From 9 months babies usually first regard a new toy appraisingly for a few moments, as if to judge its qualities, before reaching for it, and they enjoy manipulating one toy at a time. A little later, from imitation or discovery, they can combine two objects in some active way, such as banging a couple of wooden spoons together or rattling a spoon in a cup. During this time, baby is beginning to develop an ability to differentiate between familiar people and unfamiliar strangers. Object permanence develops around 9–10 months, as baby will lift a cushion to look underneath it for a half-hidden play object. It is not long after that a developed ability exists to detect a hidden object. During this time, babies enjoy producing

9 months Sitting competently on the floor, baby reaches sideways to take the pegs from their holes but is not yet able to replace them.

9 months Although not yet able to release the blocks into the cup, baby has some notion of the nature of the container and keeps on trying.

the simultaneous noise and tactile sensation of banging or sliding solid objects. All babies, as they become more mobile, increasingly seek proximity to their primary caregiver partly for the reassurance of constant availability and partly to seek co-operation in play.

From 9–12 months, babies begin to understand the import of the primary caregiver's spoken communications: first the cadences of vocal intonation, then of a few single-word forms and eventually of the simply phrased instructions and boundaries in recurrent situational contexts. Babies begin to find meaning in their homely world

9 months Having watched a playmate build a tower of blocks to knock over, baby tries to imitate. Grasping right hand and pointing left index finger are well shown.

10 months Creeping towards an eye-catching plaything and reaching for it.

and like to watch and listen to familiar adults, be touched, talked to and played with. The attention, relationships and play of the baby are still engaged and satisfied mainly at the level of ongoing perceptions, but immediate, brief imitations indicate the possession of a short-term memory and baby proceeds with the establishment of a long-term memory-bank. For the latter, all sorts of memories become stored, related to significant somatic, cognitive and affective experiences, for the purpose of instantaneous recognition, retrieval and creative assembly when needed.

Early play remains repetitive unless the primary caregiver indicates the next step. In these homely ways, a child learns during the first year that things keep their properties even in movement, but the behaviour of people tends to be unpredictable. Babies must be able to move about their familiar world so as to acquire a working knowledge of its nature and its possibilities while learning to control their own behaviours and relationships within it, before they can communicate wishes, attitudes and intentions with regard to it. Babies are also able to recognize situational constancy in home surroundings. For instance, they know when the primary caregiver is out of sight for a short time, and they begin to tolerate extended intervals of time and space between themselves and the primary caregiver.

10 months Enjoying the simultaneous sight and sound made by sliding plastic pastry cutters on the table.

11 months Having acquired the ability to crawl, baby explores their environment.

At home, babies balance a need for close proximity to the primary caregiver with a need to explore, nicely integrating motor activity with sensory alertness and emotional satisfaction. In the first 12 months baby has already travelled a far distance from early dominance by neonatal reflexes, to present individualistic manifestations of capability and personality. To achieve full potential baby must be supported to travel even further and more rapidly during the next couple of years.

11 months Baby improves their skill in locomotion by carrying two objects simultaneously.

■ Acquires hand-release skill and can now pass objects from hand to hand and drop things voluntarily.

■ Understands the permanence of objects.

■ Can tolerate short intervals of time away from the primary caregiver but will seek proximity for reassurance and co-operation in play.

■ Begins to manipulate individual objects.

■ Some brief imitative behaviour begins to emerge and baby will enjoy banging, rattling and sliding solid objects.

Key observations

In this period children become increasingly mobile, inquisitive and wilful. They have an increased ability to attend to detail and a growing recognition of cause and effect. The child is no longer satisfied with mainly perceptual phenomena and quickly loses interest in events which are presented mainly as distant, repetitious or unrewarding. This understanding is first manifest through their own experiences, and actions. The child is dominated by an urge to explore and exploit the surrounding environment: for example, when exploring cupboards, to manipulate, smell and taste the objects within, sometimes presenting them to the primary caregiver. Children at this stage are also able to manipulate blocks with a good pincer grasp.

12-18 months

Percussion tools are still employed to experiment in the synchronization of sound and strike; and with increasing skill in upright

11 months First steps require caregiver encouragement and considerable courage.

12 months Holding on to the furniture and stepping sideways, they cruise about the room, investigating objects of interest.

14 months Having gained some appreciation of the phenomenon of container and contained, they greatly enjoy putting objects in and out of the wastepaper bin.

12 months Holds the pencil in an age-typical fashion. A few moments later the pencil was shifted to the other hand.

ambulation and navigation, the child is able to push and pull large wheeled toys and guide small ones by hand or on the end of a string. Young children during this period are still tied to everyday family realities where role play features in short episodes. They also begin to communicate needs and feelings quite effectively in a medley of

12 months This give-and-take play involved not only playthings but linguistic interchange.

12 months Having thrown out all the playthings, they call loudly to get them back.

large expressive gestures, loud, tuneful vocalizations and a small but ever-increasing repertoire of single words, while showing a growing interest in naming objects and pictures, in repeating words and in listening to people talking.

At this developmental stage of limited cognitive, social and language appreciation, a doll or animal toy is treated like any other plaything. For the child, objects hold no true emotional significance, owing to immature preoccupation with the 'me' and only very primitive realization of the 'not me'. Consequently, so far as the child is concerned, young babies (who do not 'intend' anything) are not personalities in their own right, but merely objects. Social learning is undoubtedly entirely ego-centred at first: that is, 'self-tied', rather than 'self-ish'. Acceptable externalized or 'detached-from-self' activities, leading later to the practice of unselfishness, sharing, taking turns and eventually to compassionate behaviour, do not, indeed cannot, develop until a child has learned first the primary distinction of 'me' and 'not me', then the distinction of 'me' and 'you', and finally the distinction of 'us' and 'them', which is the keystone of social communication. Some of this learning depends upon appreciation of what is 'mine' and what is 'not mine', and of what is 'yours' and 'theirs'.

12 months They cannot yet name these objects but they are well able to demonstrate their use in relation to the self.

12 months Shows a vague notion of the objects' application outside of the self.

12 months This interest in books is greatly encouraged by the caregiver.

13 months The puppet evokes delighted pointing and loud vocalization.

15 months They now clearly understand the functions of a comb and speak a recognizable version of the word.

Until this final stage of cognitive and emotive maturation has been reached the child's egocentricity leads to the unshakeable conviction that all things rightfully belong to the child. As soon as children are mobile they should be provided with some playthings and a place (for territory) so that they may learn not only the satisfactions but the accepted conventions of personal and territorial possession, including the need to respect the rights of others.

Key observations

■ Increased mobility widens opportunities for exploration.

■ There is less repetitive action and increasing attention to object detail.

15 months They cannot quite link up these train carriages.

15 months Squatting on the floor, they study the picture book with interest, but turn several pages at a time.

■ Enjoyment of push-and-pull toys indicates some recognition of cause and effect.

■ Can communicate needs and wishes using an increasing repertoire of words and gestures.

■ Remains relatively egocentric and unable to separate 'me' from 'not me'.

18-24 months

Between 18 and 24 months, with rapidly improving control of the body and limbs, a child engages in many gross-motor activities such as pushing, pulling and carrying large objects, as well as climbing on furniture, low walls and steps. Sitting on a small tricycle, the child can steer it on course, but propels it forward with feet on the ground. A sense of danger, like understanding and use of language, is still very limited. However, a desire for independent action is boundless. Therefore, the child requires constant supervision to be protected from danger.

The child becomes increasingly interested in the nature and detailed exploitation of small objects, constantly practising and refining manipulative abilities. Young children will play contentedly at floor level for prolonged periods with suitable, durable toys, provided they know that a familiar and attentive adult is near. The child will enjoy putting small toys in and out of containers and is able to build towers

20 months Enjoys the simultaneous sight and sound and muscular precision of the hammering activity.

20 months An irresistible urge to get in and out of large boxes, perhaps learning their relative size and position.

18 months They walk backwards and sideways, pulling and steering a trolley containing a collection of bricks.

18 months Discovering control of a push-and-pull toy.

of blocks, varying from 3 at 18 months to 6 or more at 2 years. Children are able to experiment for lengthening periods of time with water and sand, or malleable materials like clay and dough, using their hands and simple tools effectively, but as yet without the ability to plan or achieve an end-product.

Drawings have no real pictorial representation and although one hand is tending to show dominance, such preference is still very

18 months Crawling swiftly up the garden steps. (The usual sequence of movements – right hand, left foot; left hand, right foot – is clearly shown.)

18 months Playing with the same toys as three months earlier, they are now able to link the train carriages.

2 years Having competently assumed this position, they delightedly call attention to the facts and implications of the situation.

2 years Having successfully linked up the trucks, they pull the whole train through the doorway, walking backwards and round the corner.

variable; the child continues to use either hand freely and sometimes both together. These manifestations of unequal, shifting or perhaps non-simultaneous appreciation and control of laterality continue with decreasing frequency throughout the pre-school years.

The child is still ego-centric but is actively building memories from mimicking the behaviours of those around them. Role play and situational 'pretend' play, which are characteristic of this stage, might involve the child using materials that are readily to hand. For example, nearby cushions and coverings might be used opportunistically while the child plays for a few moments at pretending to go to bed. The child is able to put two or three toys together meaningfully – a doll on a chair; bricks in a truck – but seldom, as yet, makes one object represent another or uses mime to symbolize absent things or events.

From 15–18 months onwards a child also becomes increasingly interested in picture books, first to recognize and name people, animals, objects and familiar actions (eating and drinking, getting into a car, posting a letter). Soon they can follow a simple story read aloud while exploring the pictures. Next they begin to make comments and ask questions. Some of this love of books and stories, which is very beneficial for language development, is associated with a continued need for close proximity to the primary caregiver, a normal phase of socialization.

By 18 months the child usually speaks a few single words, such as 'tup' (cup) and 'dink' (drink), in appropriate context as well as a number of meaningful utterances (holophrases) which, to the child, are single words, such as 'gimme' (give me) and 'hee-ya' (here you are); action is linked to what is being said. About 21 months the child begins to put two or more 'real' words together to frame little sentences. These usually refer to very familiar matters, or to needs and happenings in the 'here and now'. The child is now able to

2½ years Having tried unsuccessfully to step into the train, they are still a little confused regarding the relative size of truck and teddy.

2 years Medical role play.

communicate effectively wishes, refusal, likes and dislikes through a combination of gestures, and may include a few words and phrases. The child can comprehend most simple language they hear.

Also at about 21 months children begin to demonstrate their appreciation that miniature (i.e. dolls'-house-size) toys represent things and people in the real world. They clearly show this externalization (or expression) of previously internalized (i.e. memorized) experiences by spontaneously arranging the little toys in meaningful groups, by actively indicating their use in everyday situations, and often by simultaneously talking about them.

Constant sympathetic, but non-stressful adult encouragement to engage in every sort of spontaneous play is essential not only to the contentment but to the fundamental learning of children between 1 and 2 years of age. Through manipulation of playthings, they first discover through their visual, auditory and tactile perceptions what they are and what special properties they possess (i.e. their special quality), then go on to learn what can be done with them (i.e. their special function) and finally how objects can be adapted to suit their own requirements, constructional or make believe (their potentialities). This investigative behaviour is often evident during make-believe play.

2 years Imitative role play developing into inventive make believe.

21 months The beginnings of clearly representative play with miniature toys.

1¼–2¼ years Parallel play using musical instruments in a day nursery.

2½ years The bag provides endless opportunities for exploration, manipulation and imitation.

2½ years Threading beads maintains the child's interest now fingers have acquired sufficient skill.

Key observations

■ Concentration span increases and desire for independence grows.

■ Now that the child is familiar with objects within their environment, they begin to utilize them in play.

■ There is simple imitative role play of familiar scenes (i.e. mum and baby).

■ Engages in play with miniature objects but objects are used realistically and not symbolically (i.e. toy bricks might be placed into a toy truck).

■ There is a growing interest in print and mark-making activity.

2-3 years

From the age of 2 years a child is becoming increasingly skilful in every form of motor activity and may be able to ride a tricycle forwards, using the pedals, and steer it round corners. Skills of kicking, throwing and catching a ball increase.

Children's manipulations and constructive skills steadily improve and they are able to hold a pencil halfway down the shaft or near the point, scribbling or imitating to and fro lines and circles on a sheet of paper. The child enjoys simple jigsaw puzzles and can match four or five colours and several shapes.

Children instinctively use a lively form of 'total communication' composed sometimes separately but more often simultaneously of words, gestures, mime and occasionally language codemes. These developments are immediately reflected in their play. The child will still follow familiar adults around the house, imitating and joining in their activities, calling attention to their own efforts, demanding approval, and asking innumerable questions. Extending earlier role play, children invent little make-believe situations, which become

2½ years Two 'educational toys' being employed for inventive make-believe play. The man is at the top of the lighthouse.

2½ years Painting at the dining table, indifferent to the fact that the pictures are upside down.

increasingly organized and prolonged, and which they 'play out' with high seriousness. During these mini-dramas they talk aloud to themselves, in appropriate terms, describing and explaining what is being done, instructing themselves with regard to immediately forthcoming actions or formulating their uncertainties. Later they extend their inventions, adding some relevant dialogue to the role play and indicating the beginnings of forward planning, such as collecting suitable items for a dolls' tea party, or materials to construct and drive a make-believe car.

After 2½ years children's moveable 'self-space' remains chiefly relative to themselves and caregivers, but children are now prepared to admit one or two familiar children briefly into their playworld and to venture intermittently into other children's play. Although they play in close proximity, however, the play itself is mainly of the 'solo' type, so each child needs their own set of playthings and their own piece of 'territory'. At this developmental stage a child seems to realize their physical separateness before appreciating their own cognitive and affective individuality. For some time, therefore, the child remains convinced that the primary caregiver automatically apprehends what the child is feeling, needing and intending. However, under 3 years or so, the child does not expect other children to share the inner workings of their own mind, but assumes their own right to exercise dictatorial behaviour.

2½–3½ years Water play in a nursery school, providing an excellent example of parallel play. Each child has their own play materials and play space.

3½ years Gymnastics on the playground slide.

3 years The expression is full of wonder at the changing appearance of the world beneath as they swing.

3 years Enjoying the appearance and behaviour of bubbles.

Key observations

■ Role play extends to situations reflecting the wider social world (e.g. shopkeeper, doctors and nurses) and some simple narratives may begin to emerge.

■ The child might substitute one object for another in play (i.e. Lego blocks used to represent food in a mealtime scene).

■ The child can match some shapes and colours in a simple jigsaw puzzle.

■ With increased motor control, children will enjoy kicking, throwing and catching a ball.

■ May play in the proximity of other children, but solitary play is predominant and children's own space and materials are important.

■ Pencil control improves and the child may be able to copy simple circular or up-and-down marks.

3-4 years

From 3 years onwards children still need to play. The child is able to run freely, climb over and about the usual nursery apparatus, negotiate slides, crawl through barrels and jump on small trampolines. The child is able to develop skills in riding a tricycle, confidently using the pedals and steering safely round sharp corners. The child now has a clear appreciation of space in relation to their own body in size and shape, at rest and in movement. The child is able to carry large blocks, planks and boards with the help of co-operative playmates to build constructions in which to conduct a host of vivid make-believe activities.

Hand skills are also rapidly improving through play with small toys like blocks, jigsaw puzzles, miniature cars, dolls' houses and so on, and the child enjoys pencil work and cutting out shapes with scissors. Block building remains popular for many years, proceeding from simple towers to more elaborate structures, ingeniously planned and carefully executed. Children first employ blocks purely as manipulative objects, then through imitation, copying and instruction they gradually extend their forward programming or 'blueprinting' to the construction of structures which (like their spontaneous drawings) they name beforehand. Later, these constructions are often taken into other, more complicated and fanciful play with miniature cars, furniture and dolls to form part of the settings.

From 3 years onwards puzzles with a greater number of pieces are needed. It is noticeable that many children of this age are more interested in analytical fitting together of the shapes than building up the picture, so they will construct it from the plain wooden back

3½ years Simple insert jigsaw puzzles retain their fascination for much longer than one expects.

3 years Recently started nursery school, this child is still a shy onlooker.

without regard for the attractively coloured and designed front. Later assembly of a picture with many more pieces becomes all-important. It is not clear why some children perform in this fashion, but it may be that they are manifesting the commonly found sequence of learning which proceeds from general overview, through separate analysis of details, to final immediate synthesis into a well-apprehended whole.

Play with plasticine and other malleable materials can be enjoyable from 3 years onwards, and particularly with over-4s. Spontaneous drawings of 3s and 4s (as distinct from copy-design) become increasingly elaborate and diverse in colour, form and content, although they still remain chiefly concerned with people, houses, vehicles and flowers. The 3-year-old does not name the drawing until it is finished. Then, about 4 years, the child will announce beforehand what is about to be drawn, indicating some sort of preliminary 'blueprint' in thinking prior to beginning. By 4–4½ years, children may be expected to engage amicably in all sorts of self-directed play activities with peers. At this stage, improvised constructional building, table and floor games, dressing up and make-believe play are greatly favoured. Children need opportunities through play for discussion, planning, sharing, taking turns and recognition of agreed rules.

Interest in music-making, usually in the form of percussion instruments or simple wind instruments, often begins to show itself from

3 years Supremely secure, engaging in elaborate role and make-believe play.

3 years There are two participants in the dialogue, using different tones of voice and choice of words.

3½ to 4 years. Children can manifest unusually sophisticated tastes very early, not only in their listening, but in expression, recognizing and recalling tunes learned from adults and older children, or heard on the radio. Some may ask for and even manage to play such musical instruments as are within their capacity to manipulate. Meanwhile, between 3 and 4 years a child's ability to use spoken

3½ years They are well able to cope with this more complicated jigsaw puzzle, although its large size necessitated frequent unhurried contemplation.

3½ years Gracefully mounting a large, old rocking horse.

3½ years Active play merges into make-believe show jumping.

3½ years After the show jumping, the horse is fondly fed from a shopping bag.

language rapidly improves both in vocabulary and syntax so that, in spite of residual infantile mispronunciations and grammatical errors, speech is generally intelligible even to people outside the immediate family. Children and their playmates informally communicate in a glorious mixture of words, exaggerated vocal cadences, facial expressions and telling gestures, and they understand each other perfectly.

By 4 years verbal interchanges of every sort – friendly, informative, questioning, argumentative, explanatory and instructive – become increasingly evident in all aspects of play, especially in make-believe

2½–4 years Children enjoying active play in the park with their caregivers near by.

2½–4 years Young children in an adventure playground, demonstrating several interesting aspects of activity play.

3½ years Demonstrating skilful motor control and excellent spatial sense.

3 and 3½ years Children making small plasticine models of domestic and other objects.

*5½ and 3½ years
Managing a very
complicated jigsaw
puzzle, carefully
explaining their
strategies.*

situations. Once free communication has been established within any group, the signs of leadership show up clearly, with the dominant child deciding who shall play the major roles and who shall be the subsidiary characters. The leader may or may not generously agree to later interchanges of roles and taking turns. At this stage children's make-believe and subjective worlds can be so vivid to themselves that what is fact and what is fiction can become hazy; inexperienced caregivers may be startled by apparent blatant disregard for objective truth. Four-year-olds delight in rhymes, riddles, simple jokes and verbal teasing. They love having stories read to them, especially when they can simultaneously look at illustrations. Although they now appreciate peers to play with, they still enjoy being with their parents and siblings at home, continuing to learn by imitating, trying out new skills, listening, talking and asking endless questions.

By this time the child can mentally detach the physical aspects of 'self' from those of 'non-self' sufficiently well to be able to envisage the situation of hills, houses, bridges and other prominent features in the landscape from another's position in space, and they can appreciate some of the implications of visual perspective, although this does not yet appear in their drawings. They also begin to

*4½ years Handed a box of
miniature toys, the child
scrutinizes the collection* in situ
*before selecting items for
assembly. A younger child
would probably first spread
them all out on the table-top.*

*4½ years A few minutes later,
assembly is almost complete:
domestic items together, bath
'upstairs' and items of transport
'outside'.*

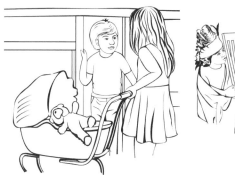 

3½ and 5 years Elaborate make-believe house play.   *3½ and 5 years Playing cowboys.*

demonstrate a growing sense of compassion and responsibility. Appetite for adventure is not always matched by appreciation of the dangers: children enjoy taking risks that end in self-discovered boundaries!

Key observations

- Children now enjoy playing with similar-aged peers.

- Role play and make believe become increasingly imaginative and complex.

- In a small social group, children learn to negotiate roles, to share and take turns.

- Increased mastery of language allows children to delight in simple jokes and rhymes.

- There is a clear appreciation of body size and shape and the child can run freely, climb, crawl and jump.

- Advanced fine motor skill facilitates more detailed drawing, and children may be able to cut out simple shapes using scissors.

- Children will enjoy the process of making things, using, for example, dough or building blocks, or gluing and sticking.

5-6 years

From this stage onwards the child steadily continues to develop everyday competence and powers of communication. In play they show an increasing enjoyment not only of elaborate make-believe activities but of complicated indoor and outdoor games which require knowledgeable preliminary instruction, hard practice, strict adherence to rules and a sense of fair play. Personal aptitudes for sports, crafts and the creative arts become ever more apparent in the child's selective use of leisure time, choice of companions and the games they play, whether at home, in playgrounds with special equipment, or in open fields and streets with no equipment at all

4½ years Coloured plastic shapes provide excellent opportunities for inventive picture-making and conversation.

4½ and 5 years At playgroup, the children collaborate in constructing an elaborate street scene complete with church, high-rise flats, flyover and traffic.

4½ years Cutting out a carpet for the dolls' house.

3–5 years Children attending a day nursery. This elaborate construction, assembled and dismantled every day, provides opportunity for every kind of outdoor play.

other than the chants and rituals of long-unwritten tradition, coupled with lively contemporary improvisations.

For the next few years the separate interests of boys and girls are clearly evident in their spontaneous play, although in school playgrounds teachers usually organize and encourage mixed-play activities.

Key observations

■ Children steadily continue to develop everyday competence and powers of communication.

■ There is an increasing enjoyment of more structured, rule-based games.

3½ and 5 years Co-operative activity play on the slide.

4 years Elaborate building with large wooden blocks involving considerable forward planning and precise construction.

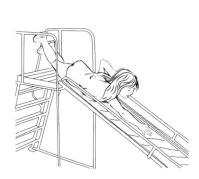

5 years Child on a slide.

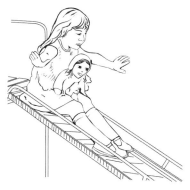

5 years Gymnastics on the slide, involving appropriate verbal instruction of the doll.

4½ years A competent performer on the trampoline.

A certain element of danger adds to the attraction of this swing.

A group of familiar friends on the roundabout in the park.

The same children performing skilfully on a more difficult roundabout (they call it 'doing Olympics').

- ■ Increased improvisational ability means play often needs minimal props and good use can be made of open-ended materials.

- ■ Personal aptitudes for sports, crafts and the creative arts become ever more apparent.

Sheridan's observations document how, as children grow, they develop new competencies that contribute to their *ability to play* in different ways. Using the secure base formed through attachment with the primary caregiver, they explore the environment, at first using their senses. Through continued interaction with others, they gradually develop communication and social skills, recognizing a world outside of the self. With mobility and dexterity, they explore objects and their properties, utilizing them in increasingly complex ways. Through this expanding repertoire of play behaviour, children learn about themselves, about others and about the world around them, *developing through play*. Beginning with early sensory experiences, through the controlled manipulation and symbolic use of objects, to imaginative make believe, children's progressive play skills offer them unique ways to experience and make sense of their world (Jennings, 1999). The pattern of 'What is this?', 'What does this do?', 'What *can* I do with this?' and 'What *could* I do with this?' is evident in possibility thinking across the lifespan (Craft, 2005).

Summary

- Spend some time considering how Sheridan's observations map on to the developmental sequences of Piaget, Parten and Erikson (described in Chapter 1).

  - What do you think are the notable advances in social, cognitive and emotional development?

- Observe a child or group of children at play.

  - How easy did you find the observation process?

- How did you decide what to observe and how to record the information?

- How do your observations fit with Sheridan's in relation to observed competencies and the child/children's age(s)?

 Give yourself some time to think

Hughes, F. (2010) *Children, Play and Development* (4th Edition). London: Sage.

Riddall-Leech, S. (2008) *How to Observe Children* (2nd Edition). Harlow: Heinemann.

 Useful reading

3

Outlines of some
particular play sequences

In the previous chapter, we presented Sheridan's original observations of children's play. Through her observations, Sheridan illustrated how play changes with age as children gradually acquire new competencies that both reflect and influence their development. We saw how play progresses from that which is sensory in nature, to symbolic play, imaginative play and play that incorporates rules. Sheridan also detailed the increasingly social nature of play.

To exemplify the changes she had noted in children's play over time, Sheridan selected observations of children using particular materials and grouped these together in 'play sequences'. We present these sequences here. As in Chapter 2, the ages noted below each illustration represent the child's age at the time of observation and are not necessarily indicative of the earliest or latest time at which behaviours might emerge. Also remain mindful that wide variation is to be expected.

The specific aims of this chapter are:

■ To outline some particular play sequences involving cup, bell and block play, mark making and small world activity.

■ To highlight, by showing children of different ages interacting with the same materials, the ways in which play changes over time.

6 months Having grasped with both hands, baby passes to one hand and brings the most prominent feature of the cup to the mouth.

9 months Grasping the cup right side up with both hands, baby brings the rim to their mouth, looking at the caregiver.

12 months Having just observed me place cup and spoon on table after testing their hearing by stroking the rim of this cup, they seize the cup and spoon and successfully imitate.

12 months The foregoing imitation reminds them of the true function of cups and spoons and they promptly offer a clear example of definition-by-use.

2¼ years Cups, spoons and other related domestic items are happily incorporated into make-believe play.

Bell play

24 weeks Grasps bell at base with both hands, obviously concentrating serious attention on activity. Immediately afterwards the top of the handle is brought to the mouth.

9 months Grasps mid-handle with one hand and delightedly bangs noisily and repeatedly on table-top.

10 months Seizes top of handle with one hand and rings bell, enjoying musical sound.

11 months Pokes at clapper with index finger.

12 months The bell shape reminds them of a cup and they act accordingly. It is difficult to decide whether this is fortuitous exploration or deferred definition-by-use.

9 months Holding a block competently in each hand, they bring them together in interested comparison. A few moments later the child found considerable pleasure in clicking them together.

12 months Having found a block hidden under the cup, the child begins to explore some further possibilities on their own account.

15 months Blocks are arranged as shown entirely by the child. They seem to be recalling some previous game of 'pushing a train' with an older playmate.

15 months The child has always enjoyed handling blocks and readily builds little towers of two or three with their right hand while grasping a larger stuffed animal toy with the left.

2 years A particularly competent young architect. Having built half the tower with their right hand, they shift attention to the left. This interesting form of self-training is very common.

3 years A fine example of previous learning using up every block to form a bridge and counting them aloud.

3½ years The caregiver is building three steps out of bricks behind a screen – a difficult 'test' at this age.

3½ years But with long experience of constructive block play the child has no difficulty in copying the model.

12 months Imitative artist at work. Typical grasp of pencil at its proximal end with right hand with 'mirror' posturing in left hand. A moment later the pencil was passed from right to left, again marking paper.

15 months Firmer grasp of the pencil now and held lower down the shaft, end product of to and fro lines and dots is improved. Mirror posture in left hand.

3½ years Interesting example of simultaneous two-handed performance. The pencil grip near tip is more mature, but the production is still non-pictorial.

21 months Larger brushwork at an easel. Productions are still more in the nature of visuo-motor activities than representative pictures.

3½ years Right-handed mature grip of pencil with non-engagement of left. The child asked to be given a letter to copy. They did not seem to realize that what had been copied was upside down.

4 years Drawing a typical age-characteristic house with cornered windows, simultaneously thinking aloud about it. The mature grip of right hand and the helpful use of left (to steady the paper) are well shown.

3½ and 4 years Painting human figures. One used only black paint, the other several colours. The end products are both fairly age-characteristic. Originally reported these as self-portraits, but cheerfully admitted many inaccuracies.

4¼ years The child produces a colourful self-portrait with numerous common environmental embellishments – yellow sun, blue sky, green trees, brown earth. They print their name beneath, working briskly and silently in happy concentration.

15 months Miniature toys are merely small items to be manipulated and put in and out of an upright box-like container.

18 months The miniature toys are objects for give-and-take play with the caregiver. The caregiver names toys and the child repeats the name, but still does not appreciate that the toys represent real-life objects.

2½ years The child knows that the toys are representative, but prefers to assemble them in smaller, separated groups outside the doll's house.

3¼ years The child plays with the miniatures inside one room of the house, carrying on a long, audible monologue for their own and their doll's benefit.

5 years Playing constructively all over the house. Although silent, they are busily engaged.

6 and 6 1/2 years 'Special friends', they said, engaged in elaborate, co-operative, make-believe play in the doll's house. The play goes on continuously from day to day. They had papered the walls and made all of the furnishings themselves.

Variation in children's play 4

Consistent with Sheridan's original focus, this chapter will consider play and atypical development. However, in addition, it will include a discussion of variation in play according to gender, culture and adversity.

The specific aims of the chapter are:

- To highlight some of the key issues relating to play according to gender, culture, atypical development and adversity.

- To consider the value of understanding variation apparent in play in relation to professional play practice and providing for play.

Culture

Understanding variation in play is important because it provides an insight into the uniqueness of different cultures, facilitates culturally appropriate professional practice, and highlights the dynamic and ever-changing structure and social organization of families (Roopnarine *et al.*, 1998). Through her observations, Sheridan demonstrates how children develop a repertoire of play behaviours, this repertoire growing with children's increasing social, physical, intellectual and emotional competencies. Children across all cultures play in the ways described by Sheridan, developing a repertoire of skills to support play that involves the use of senses, objects, symbolism and pretence, and an understanding of rules. As Hughes (2010) states, play is a true cultural universal and even children with substantial domestic or agricultural duties seem to find opportunities to play during their day (Maybin and Woodhead, 2003). However, although there appears no cultural variation in the development of children's *ability to play*, culture both influences and is manifested in children's *play behaviour*. Variation that exists in children's play behaviour both within and across cultures is likely to reflect the way adults interact with their children, with the emphasis placed on the value and function of play and the play environment.

As has been previously noted, parents or primary caregivers often serve as a baby's first playmate. The literature surrounding parenting behaviour suggests that cultural variations exist in the nature of early interactions between children and their primary caregivers (Darling and Steinberg, 1993). Of importance to the process of developing play skills, however, is that effective early parent–child interactions serve to ensure that the child feels emotionally secure and able to explore their social and material environment. Lieberman (1977) talked of parents and teachers as 'cultural surrogates', inhibiting or encouraging children's play. In a review of the literature on parent–child interaction during play, O'Reilly and Bornstein (1993) demonstrated that the level of sophistication in children's play was related to the quality and nature of early parent–child interactions. Effective early interactions are characterized by the provision of boundaries and emotional responsiveness. Darling and Steinberg (1993) remind us that parenting occurs within a cultural context, and the way that parents express emotional responsiveness and set boundaries in play often reflects parenting practice which itself is deeply embedded within a cultural context. Hughes (2010) describes how American mothers tend to set broad boundaries in play, encouraging children to take notice of and explore the wider environment, consistent with their promotion of autonomy and independence. By contrast, he describes how Japanese mothers tend to encourage play that involves close and controlled social interaction, such as nurturing doll play, promoting a sense of dependency. Haight *et al.* (1999) also describe how the themes of pretend play reflect socialization goals: for example, European and American caregivers emphasize individuality, self-expression and independence, while Chinese caregivers emphasize harmonious social interaction, obedience, respect and rules.

The transmission of cultural values through play is also evident in the emphasis placed on play within education. In China, play has traditionally been seen as recreational rather than educational and not related to intellectual development (Cooney and Sha, 1999). Whereas messy play areas are common to early years classrooms in the United Kingdom, David and Powell (2005) found that Chinese practitioners failed to understand why an area that encouraged children to get dirty should be promoted as it contradicted the principles of cleanliness and order.

Variation also exists in the availability or suitability of play materials. Lindon (2001) describes how, in some cultures, dolls hold particular spiritual or ceremonial significance and as such might not be considered suitable for play. Where toys are not available for play, children will often construct what they need from materials found in their environment. Play materials in Kenya among Massai children, for example, include toys made from wood, straw, animal skins and bone, stones, and other found objects. Sometimes props are not needed at all and play revolves solely around shared knowledge and understanding (Haight *et al.*, 1999): for example, in the development of game-playing rules in street culture (Sobel, 2001). At the other end of the spectrum, the influence of our technological world is reflected in the replica toys made available for even the youngest children: for example, pretend mobile phones and baby laptops. The miniaturization of the technology associated with consumer electronics means that children may now interact with sophisticated materials as they play.

Globalization and an increasingly multicultural society are also reflected in children's play. The festivities associated with Halloween, a celebration that involves dressing up as ghosts and ghouls and playing such games as apple-bobbing and trick or treat, originated in American culture but have since spread to many other parts of the world. Play in an East Indian context is often influenced by ceremonial activities, such as the celebration of Diwali, where children and families tell ancient stories through puppetry, music and dance, and celebrate colour and light through mark making and fireworks (Roopnarine *et al.*, 1998). In a growing multicultural society, these celebrations are increasingly likely to be shared by children and families from a variety of backgrounds, through community activities and school experiences.

Gender

Gender influences and is manifested in children's play behaviour in much the same way as culture. Variation reflects adult interactions with children, children's interactions with each other as well as gendered norms and values projected through marketing and the media.

The words 'gender' and 'sex' are often used interchangeably. For example, on forms or questionnaires we may be asked to tick a box to indicate our 'gender' as being male or female. The response required, however, relates to our biological sex. Arguably, gender relates to the characteristics associated with our biological sex, characteristics which are often learned via the process of socialization. Distinguishing between sex and gender in research is important as findings relating to sex differences would suggest variation between boys and girls from a biological or genetic perspective, whereas findings relating to gender difference would include variation resulting from the process of socialization. As the development of play skills is largely a social process, unpicking that which is a result of biological sex and that which is a result of socialization can be difficult, if not impossible. If we consider the observations of Sheridan in relation to the social, physical, intellectual and linguistic competencies associated with the developing repertoire of play skills, then, from a biological perspective, boys and girls progress in much the same way. Variation is more apparent in relation to what they choose to play.

Research has consistently demonstrated that, given a choice of toys to play with, children show a preference for those that are commonly associated with their own gender: for example, girls choose to play with dolls, prams or tea-sets, while boys choose cars, trucks or building blocks (Hines and Kaufman, 1994). Servin *et al.* (1999) demonstrated that these gendered choices became apparent as early as 12 months. However, even at this young age, it is still difficult to conclude that the behaviour is a result of any differences due to biological sex. Returning to Sheridan's point about parents acting as children's first play partners, it seems likely that, in a more general sense, styles of interaction with children from birth could contribute to the development of their gendered toy preferences. Mothers and fathers have been shown to interact with their children in subtly different ways, with mothers tending towards intimate communicative forms of interaction and fathers tending towards more physical activity (Sun and Roopnarine, 1996). The gender of the child also influences the style of our interactions. Lindahl and Heimann (1997) studied the social behaviour of mother–daughter and mother–son dyads and found that mother–daughter dyads remained in closer proximity to one another and engaged in more physical and visual contact. It may be that the close proximity and intimate communication apparent in interaction with baby girls lends itself to nurturing types of play while the emphasis on physical activity and opportunities for independence and exploration are reflected in boys choosing to play with mobile toys, such as cars and trucks.

Interestingly, gendered differences in day-to-day parent–child interactions reduce with age, perhaps because they have served their purpose in provoking children's initial awareness of being male or female. However, Lindsey *et al.* (2010) found that, despite showing no gender differences in day-to-day caregiver interaction, parents continued to engage in gendered patterns of behaviour with their children during play. Rogoff (2003) explains that young children actively develop their understanding of gender through play, exploring the concepts of 'boy' and 'girl' and acting out the extremes of each role. As well as imitating what they see in their home environments, a widened social network coupled with exposure to television broadcasting reinforces their gender knowledge. Differences are manifest within more complex types of play, for example in the types of role-playing games in which they choose to engage and in the specific roles they adopt within this play. The patterns of preferential toy choice made in the first year extend into later childhood, where girls seek out information about human relationships and boys seek out action (Kalliala, 2006). Boys' tendency to engage in more rough-and-tumble activity is perhaps the most widely documented gender variation in children's play. Research has consistently shown that across cultures, boys tend to engage in more of this physical type of play than girls (Jarvis, 2006). Themes in role play among boys also tend to involve war or pseudo-violence, and much has been done in the United Kingdom to curtail this type of activity. However, there is no clear evidence that engagement in combat play leads to future violence (Holland, 2003) and, as we saw in the previous section, children are likely to follow their desired play patterns even in the absence of props, either doing without or making toys out of found items.

Adversity and atypicality

It seems unlikely that variation in the spontaneous development of children's play behaviour is directly influenced by gender or culture. While the content of their play may differ, boys and girls across many cultures develop the physical, cognitive, social and linguistic capacities to play in the variety of ways described by Sheridan. Any differences in the predominance of play behaviour according to gender or culture, in the main, appear to emerge as a result of environmental stimuli and the assimilation of cultural norms and values: for example, through the availability of materials, parenting behaviour, peer interaction or exposure to the media. Observations of children's play among those facing severe adversity or those who have particular developmental needs may be more likely to indicate different or disrupted patterns of play behaviour.

Sheridan describes how, with adequate opportunity and support, children gain mastery over their actions, integrating sensory and motor experiences. This mastery builds esteem and confidence, and children spontaneously seek out new challenges. They use their existing play skills and emotional security as resources to support future development. Adversity and atypicality can alter or interrupt this process.

In the case of adversity, children may not be provided with the opportunity to play or to create a strong emotional base through secure attachments. Webb and Brown (2003) demonstrated how regular interaction with others and being offered opportunities to play greatly improved the development of children who had previously been confined to hospital beds in Romania. Alternatively, children may face such severe disruption that the prospect of a new challenge overwhelms them and they may stop playing or return to early play behaviours with which they feel comfortable. According to Hyder (2005), the majority of children can be helped to overcome adversity through their own play. After the 2006 Lebanese war, UNICEF funded the development of recreational areas to restore children's play behaviours and found that reintroducing opportunities to play in a safe space contributed greatly to children's well-being. Of course, for some children, specialist support is necessary and complex trauma might involve children working with play therapists or psychotherapists. Here, play is employed more directly as a means of communicating and resolving emotional issues.

Atypically developing children may have physical disabilities, sensory, social or intellectual impairment or a combination of these things, which makes integrating learning experiences more challenging. Writing about deaf children, Marschark (1993) suggests that in a bid to view disability more positively, we can often dismiss what he terms self-evident truths, in that atypically developing children often experience a more limited world, their interactions are guided by different rules and constraints and these differences are likely to impact on their development in complex and numerous ways. He proposes that the key issue is to look beyond superficial differences to those that have functional significance, those that impact on children's development and subsequent life experiences. From a developmental perspective, children with sensory, social and intellectual impairments often show a preference for more solitary or parallel types of play and engage in less imaginative role play or symbolic play with objects (Hughes, 2010). More important than observing differences in children's play patterns, however, is understanding why these differences occur, whether these differences are likely to impact on achievement, enjoyment and quality of life and, if so, whether support based on children's abilities can be tailored to broaden skills and experiences. Unpacking the social, cognitive, linguistic and physical demands of play and reflecting on children's potential to meet these demands mean we are better able to provide play opportunities that are appropriately challenging but do not risk frustration, boredom or emotional distress.

Children can be helped to overcome adversity and to make the most of their play with considered support that builds on their strengths and abilities. Considered support will undoubtedly involve parents and professionals working with children in partnership, providing for enjoyment of the here and now of play, as well as supporting developmental progress. Sheridan remarks that 'some of the so-called play pressed upon atypically developing children, always with the best intention, has been perilously close to drudgery' (1977, p. 13). It is important that we do not overemphasize play as a way of becoming, at the detriment to play as a way of being (Sturrock *et al.*, 2004). We must remain mindful that a sense of freedom, choice and control is paramount to the broad range of play experiences we offer to all children (Howard, 2010b).

Inclusive play practice

Sheridan's observations of real children engaged in their own spontaneous play reveal how social, physical, linguistic and cognitive competencies gradually accrue, to enable increasingly complex forms of play. Development of and through play reflects the increasingly effective integration of sensory and motor experiences, and these experiences are supported by social interaction. Information based on developmental milestones often feeds into targets for attainment, and it has been argued that this emphasizes a top-down or deficit model of development that focuses on the skills children have yet to achieve, rather than their current abilities (Lindon, 2001). However, understanding the skills associated with children's behaviour is important even in a bottom-up approach. At a basic level it allows us to plan the experiences and materials we might make available for children; but, importantly, it also helps us to understand and support their development better. The *Birth to Three Matters* agenda (DfES, 2002) suggests that development is best supported through play as it enables children to explore the world around them and offers rich opportunities for social interaction. However, enabling children to learn through play relies on our understanding that play itself is a developmental process and, like other developmental processes, is subject to variation. Play behaviours and play skills can be indicative of and/or influenced by culture, atypicality and adversity. Best practice recognizes children's growing *ability to play* as well as supporting their *development through play*.

Throughout this book we have been reminded that while children learn in lots of different ways, the sense of freedom, choice and control inherent in play renders it particularly useful for development. When children are at play, their development is enhanced. Remaining mindful of these characteristics can ensure inclusive and supportive play practice. Most notably, good practice starts with the child and emphasizes achievement rather than attainment (DfES, 2001). If we seek to promote activities that afford a sense of freedom, choice and control, we can be more certain that our practice begins with the child. We can support children's application of what they know and can do, fostering their personal learning journeys. Inclusive play practice is accessible to all children and allows them to demonstrate achievement, whatever their ability. As will be discussed in the following chapter, adults have an important role in supporting children's play experiences. They make decisions as to the time, space and materials made available for safe play, accommodating and supporting children's repertoire of play skills. They recognize the value of children's own initiated activities and understand factors that might influence or be manifested in children's play. They negotiate their position as a play partner, responding sensitively to children's play cues to maintain or extend the play flow. Supporting children's *ability to play*, as well as promoting their *development through play*, involves constant reflection.

Establishing a partnership with the child and their family ensures that we begin planning play experiences with as much knowledge as possible. Information can be shared across multidisciplinary teams and might consider:

- cultural values and beliefs;
- family structure;
- strengths and challenges: social, physical, cognitive, linguistic and emotional;
- likes and dislikes;
- any issues of adversity.

Information gained from talking to the child, their parents or other professionals is combined with expertise in child development and play, to guide planning and provision. This might consider:

- What kinds of experiences will best support the child? Why?
- What kinds of activities and materials are suitable? Why?

- Do planned experiences support ability to play as well as development through play?

- Do the experiences afford the child a sense of freedom, choice and control?

- What will your role be in these activities and how will this be managed?

Once play is ongoing, a constant process of reflection informs developmental progress, future planning and our own professional development. This might include planned, opportunistic, structured or unstructured observations and talking to children about their play, perhaps using photographs or artefacts as conversational prompts. It might involve thinking about time, space and materials for play or about our own role in play activities. Some questions to ask might include:

- How enjoyable or desirable are the activities?

- How are spaces and materials being used?

- Is the child able to employ current skills? Can they develop new ones?

- How do the observations feed into knowledge of the child in relation to previously noted strengths and weaknesses?

- What was your role in the play? Was this as planned? Was it effective?

Summary

- All children seem to engage in play.

- Play reflects cultural norms and values.

- Socialization can influence children's play preferences.

- Play can help children to overcome adversity.

- Inclusive play practice fosters ability to play as well as development through play.

- Take some time to research a culture that is different to your own.

  – Do you find anything that might impact on children's play or your own play practice?

- Next time you are watching television or reading a magazine, look out for gendered information.

  – Towards whom is the material directed?

  – What impact might this have on children's developing gender identity?

 Give yourself some time to think

Fromberg, D. and Bergen, D. (2006) *Play from Birth to Twelve: Contexts, Perspectives and Meaning*. Sussex: Routledge.
Hyder, T. (2005) *War, Conflict and Play*. Maidenhead: Open University Press.
Macintyre, C. (2009) *Play for Children with Special Needs*. Sussex: Routledge.

Useful reading

5   Providing for play

This chapter will focus on the ways in which children's development can be supported through play. Extending our discussion of reflective practice from the previous chapter, we will consider the role of adults in play, including parents or primary caregivers, along with a variety of different play professionals who may be encountered by children as they grow.

The specific aims of the chapter are:

- To consider provision for play in relation to adult roles, playmates and resources.
- To explore the roles of different play professions and the theoretical underpinnings of these roles.

Provisions for play

Sheridan (1977) identifies four provisions as being of primary importance to enable spontaneous play: playthings, playspace, playtime and playmates.

Sheridan (1977) writes:

- *Playthings* must be appropriate for the child's age and stage of growth and development. Not too few or the child will lack stimulation, and not too many or they will become confused and unable to concentrate.

- *Playspace* is needed for the 'free-ranging' activities which are commonly shared with others, but every child must also possess a small personal 'territory' which they know is their own and provides a secure home base.

- *Playtime* must be reasonably peaceful and predictable. It should be adequate for fulfilment of whatever activity is engaging the child's interest, without premature interruption likely to cause frustration, or undue prolongation leading to boredom, loneliness or feeling of neglect.

- *Playfellows* are required at all stages of development. Encouraging adults are not only essential to dependent infants but also in the period of *solo-play* which is characteristic of children under 2½ years, who are still unaware of such abstract principles as equal rights, sharing and taking turns. The need for companionship proceeds as social communications improve.

In commercial society, we can often feel overwhelmed with toys designed to have pre-planned outcomes that promote cultural materialistic values. Items with such fixed purposes often appear to contradict the notion of spontaneity in play. Indeed, sometimes these items place a strong emphasis on developmental or educational outcomes rather than offering real play value. Hyun (1998) suggests that parents from European and North American backgrounds often value play for its potential to promote cognitive development and that this influences them when choosing toys for their children. However, in Chapter 1, we saw how the same activity could be seen as play or not play by children, where the approach taken to the activity is more important than the materials themselves. Children's playthings are often the simplest of items, objects that can be used flexibly in a variety of ways. Fabrics of different colours and textures stimulate the senses and at the same time provide endless ideas for dressing up. As Sheridan demonstrates in her observations, cardboard boxes can be climbed into and out of as children learn about their relative size, and they can be used to make dens or other constructions. Children can make great use of household items and will often choose these over plastic imitations, preferring real saucepans and spoons in their imitative domestic play. Saucepans and spoons are also ideal for noise making. Random collections of

Playthings

items in a box or basket *invite* rather than *direct* the young child to explore objects and their properties (Goldschmied and Jackson, 1994). Children being creative with items that are not restricted by a particular use is also framed within Nicholson's theory of loose parts (1971). This emphasizes the value of offering children open-ended and often natural play materials that give them the opportunity to develop their play – introducing, modifying and changing ideas. When choosing materials for play, it is useful to consider their purpose and play value and their potential for open and closed use. Of course, materials must always be safe for children and checked frequently for wear and tear.

Time and space

When creating time and space for play, it is useful to be aware that children become attuned to details such as where, when and with whom activities take place, and they learn to distinguish play from other activities through their experiences (Howard, 2002). To encourage children to take a playful approach to a wide range of activities, adults can ensure that play is not restricted to a particular location, unnecessarily timed, socially prescriptive or secondary to other activities. Time available for play need not be excessive and children seek out opportunities to play amid the busiest of schedules. If children are in control of their play, the potential for them to become bored, restless or prematurely interrupted is kept to a minimum.

Sheridan stresses the importance of both shared and personal spaces for children's play. Children need space where they can play with others but also smaller, quiet spaces for their own solitary activity, providing opportunities for autonomy and independence but also a secure base to which they can return or retreat, as and when necessary. Indoor and outdoor places are both important. Children seek adventure and challenge in their play outdoors; they explore places and enjoy transforming spaces to create imaginary worlds (Tovey, 2007). A particular challenge is providing play spaces that stimulate children's abilities within the boundaries of health, safety and wellbeing (NCB, 1998).

Living and learning with others are essential skills for life. As is documented in Chapter 1, play becomes increasingly social over time. Interacting with others in play increases children's social skills, an awareness of self and an awareness of norms and values.

Partners in play

A newborn baby is able to communicate and respond to their mother's voice, face, touch, taste and smell. Mothers appear inherently prepared to respond to their babies, form a lasting attachment, and are sensitive to their babies' needs. Spontaneous play often involves primary carers being the baby's best toy. Early interactions encourage social interaction and playfulness, for example peek-a-boo and imitation games. Early relationships are particularly important for the development of attachments which enable the young child to feel secure enough to explore their world. Recent large-scale research has demonstrated the importance of high-quality adult–child interactions for children's development in the early years (Sylva *et al.*, 2004). Quality parent–child interaction involves listening to, respecting and supporting the child to encourage an exploration of strengths and limitations within secure boundaries.

Parents/carers and siblings

Friendship longevity develops over time. Young children often refer to playmates as their friends. For example, when a 3-year-old says, 'I am your friend now,' it probably means 'I am playing with you now' (Dowling, 2000). Children develop a closeness to friends interested in playing the same games through shared play experiences. Initial friendship choices are based on proximity and being playmates. During this play, however, children develop the skills necessary to learn about themselves and others, enabling them to make friendship decisions based on personal characteristics.

Peers and friendships

Lindon (2001) identifies the important roles adopted by adults in play, including:

Other adults

- Play partner – becoming an equal in the play.
- Observer – observing children's development and progress.
- Admirer – showing that you value the play.
- Facilitator – easing play along.

- Model – showing how play materials might be used.

- Mediator – resolving conflict.

- Safety officer – ensuring safety.

Taking on a range of roles is important. A predominantly mediating or modelling role can influence whether children accept adults into their play on future occasions (Howard, 2002). Engaging as an equal partner in play affords children an authentic sense of control and communicates that we value their own directed activities. The nature of the dialogue that occurs is also important. Particular types of question posing can enable possibility thinking and creativity (Chappell *et al.*, 2008) and teachers who use open-ended questions and authentic dialogue are more likely to be accepted by children as play partners (Howard and McInnes, 2010)

Stepping back and listening to the child offers empowerment; the child is in a position to take control in decision-making, rather than following the adult's decisions. Being sensitive, showing respect and taking an empathetic stance will allow the practitioner and child to establish a trusting relationship. The child will feel sufficiently safe to take risks that are framed by a shared understanding of boundaries.

Play in different contexts

The opportunities for development within authentic play activities cannot be neatly compartmentalized. Play supports children's development across multiple domains.

Sheridan (1977) writes:

Play provides opportunities to strengthen the body, improve the mind, develop the personality and acquire social competence, it is as necessary as food, warmth and protective care. It represents:

- *Apprenticeship*, i.e. practice leading to competence in everyday skills.

- *Research*, i.e. observation, exploration, speculation and discovery.

- *Occupational therapy*, i.e. relief from pain, boredom or distress.

- *Recreation*, i.e. simple, enjoyable fun

Opportunities for apprenticeship, research, occupational therapy and recreation exist in all play, particularly when children are afforded freedom, choice and control. However, various play professionals emphasize opportunities differently. For example, the educational value of play has traditionally focused far more on the role of play for exploration, discovery and the development of skills, features of Sheridan's apprenticeship and research roles.

One of the first advocates of play in early education was Froebel (1782–1852). Froebel designed particular materials to support what he described as the occupation of play. As a result, his ideas are often interpreted as being structured and focused on skills development. This was certainly true for Montessori (1870–1952), who developed sets of apparatus to stimulate physical and sensory ability. Froebel, however, argued that play was the highest form of human expression and paid particular attention to the importance of open-ended play experiences for supporting personal and emotional development. Isaacs (1932) shared this view, and argued that the autonomy afforded to children in play supported a positive sense of self which, in turn, promoted intellectual development. Publishing in the same era, Piaget, who argued that play was secondary to real learning, became better known. He suggested that children's development could be documented in stages and that particular abilities and ways of thinking begin to emerge at key times. Of importance was that this pattern of development would unfold without the need for instruction and that children benefited from being active in their own learning. His focus on the nature of cognition, while invaluable for increasing knowledge of child development, translated into age-related practices

Educational play

and the need for activities to work towards promoting children's achievement of particular skills. His emphasis on the child's active role translated into discovery-based learning techniques but inadvertently led to a rather redundant role for practitioners.

Vygotsky (1978) placed stronger emphasis on the social and cultural elements of play. He suggested that play served as the first form of language and communication and that during play children learned to understand the nature of rules and symbols. Social interaction was of particular importance and his notion of a zone of proximal development suggested that adults and more competent peers were able to support children's learning, enabling the completion of more complex tasks that they would eventually be able to complete alone. Although Vygotsky emphasized the social nature of learning, for him, children's own play activity served as a facilitator, much like the adult or more competent peer. Indeed, he argued that, in play, children behave as though they are a head taller than themselves.

The ideas of Piaget and Vygotsky are synthesized in the work of Bruner (1960). Heavily influenced by Piaget, Bruner proposed three different modes of exploration in early childhood:

- Enactive – direct manipulation of objects.

- Iconic – mental manipulation of objects.

- Symbolic – abstract manipulation of symbols.

Bruner challenged the Piagetian idea that children needed to be ready for certain types of learning. He suggested that almost any concept could be introduced to children in some form at any time, and that the three different modes of exploration could be used without restriction. He argued that children needed to develop fundamental learning skills rather than facts, and that the best way to do this was via repeated exposure to basic ideas. In this spiral approach, children are able to extend their thinking, accruing skills and abilities that they can transfer to different contexts.

The proposition that children's learning is best supported by certain continuous learning opportunities as well as more directed tasks is echoed in current curricula initiatives in the United Kingdom, such as the Foundation Phase in Wales (DCELLS, 2008) and the Foundation Stage in England (DCSF, 2008b). There is also more widespread recognition that the freedom and choice inherent in play supports children's emotional and intellectual growth (Laevers, 1994).

Play therapy grew from the psychoanalytic tradition of Freud (1856–1939). Anna Freud developed her father's ideas, documenting the benefits of play to establish a relationship between the therapist and the child that could facilitate the process of psychotherapy. In addition, she suggested children used play to replay events and explore ways of dealing with emotions. Melanie Klein placed even greater emphasis on the interpretation of children's play as being indicative of conflict or crises. A major criticism of psychoanalytic play therapy is the notion that play is representative of the unconscious mind and requires interpretation. There are real dangers associated with mis/over-interpretation or, indeed, whether any level of interpretation is warranted. Winnicott (1971) suggested that the process of play was far more important. This, coupled with the emergence of more humanistic approaches to therapy, has led to a variety of play therapy practices that are distinct from the psychoanalytic tradition, each involving different degrees of adult direction and interpretation (see Wilson and Ryan, 2005).

Therapeutic play

The value placed by Sheridan on children's spontaneous play accords with the non-directive approach developed by Axline (1989). This emphasizes both the significance of the play process and the importance of a warm and accepting therapeutic relationship. This approach is guided by eight principles that ensure the child feels their own initiated play activities are valued. The therapist recognizes this by reflecting back to the child what is being done, showing they are present and aware. There is acknowledgement but not praise, which ensures that the play proceeds in the way the child wishes, rather than promoting any compliance to social desirability. Whereas therapies following the psychoanalytic tradition can be difficult to evidence, more support is available for the beneficial effects of this non-directive approach. The non-directive approach supports not only children's emotional needs but the development of play skills. After ten sessions of non-directive play therapy, Trostle (1988) observed not only improvements in children's emotional health but more complex imaginative play.

There are parallels between non-directive play therapy and good practice in other professional contexts. Emphasis is placed on the play process and the naturally occurring therapeutic effects children's own spontaneous play activity can offer. Arguably, any setting where children are allowed to play freely, following their own intention, will offer the therapeutic effects encompassed in Axline's approach. This underpins the proposition of Hyder (2005), who argues that, for many children, the challenge of adversity can often be met with opportunities to play rather than therapy.

Recreational play

Cohen (2006) suggests that the provision of recreational play spaces such as parks and playgrounds grew out of initiatives designed for social engineering. He describes how playgrounds were initially provided to keep children off the streets, offering places where they could engage in purposeful physical and social activity. The emphasis was on needing to control children's urge to play so as to avoid moral decline. In the 1930s, however, rather than being driven by any psychological, pedagogical or social outcome, Sorenson, a Danish landscaper, questioned whether society could do more to facilitate children's play needs and designed the first junk playground. It housed waste materials such as timber, old cars and boxes.

The first adventure playground was opened in 1943 in Denmark. Following its success, there was a prolific growth in playground provision. The opportunistic visit of Lady Allen of Hurtwood to the Danish junk playground in 1946 led to the adoption of the idea in the United Kingdom. These playgrounds came to be known as adventure playgrounds and were characterized by affording children the opportunity to play as freely as possible within safe limits. The adventure playground movement recognized the need for children to satisfy their spontaneous drive to play and understood that play was necessarily child directed. Children needed outdoor spaces to take risks and try out new ideas, free from unnecessary rules and constraint. Children's ownership of the play was of principal importance, and this underpins current playwork practice.

Gill (2007) suggests opportunities for outdoor play might be reduced in modern Western society due to increased traffic, media scare stories about paedophilia and ever-increasing concerns about litigation among professionals who work with children. Support for the need to increase recreational play opportunities is evidenced by funding for provision being made available via initiatives such as the Play Strategy (DCSF, 2008a). Outdoor play is also emphasized in current early years curricula and the Forest School movement (Knight, 2009). Following a small scale study, Waters and Begley (2007) suggest that risk taking behaviours are supported by the Forest School environment as it promotes a permissive ethos towards physical challenge and offers a diverse natural environment.

The play activity that frequently occurs in outdoor spaces contributes greatly to bodily awareness, balance and co-ordination (Greenland, 2006). Tovey (2010) describes how flexible play spaces promote risk-taking behaviour and allow children to explore the unknown. She proposes that managing risk is an essential, transferable life skill. A principal benefit of outdoor play is arguably the fact that it has reduced or self-regulated boundaries, which maximize children's sense of freedom, choice and control.

The role of play professionals

Teachers and classroom assistants

Within the realms of early education, play has been described as a principal vehicle for learning and it is central to such curriculum initiatives as the Foundation Phase in Wales (DCELLS, 2008). Emphasis is placed on the development of the whole child and teachers and classroom assistants must support children's development through the indoor and outdoor play opportunities they provide. Given the amount of time children spend in the school environment, teachers and classroom assistants are arguably our most important play professionals. Their jobs require extensive knowledge of play, learning and child development, and the skills to combine this successfully with the requirements of the curriculum.

Claire, nursery nurse, UK

I've been a nursery nurse for eleven years now and I started with a BTEC National Diploma qualification. I've seen many changes to the curriculum and we are currently working with the Foundation Phase, which is a play-based approach. Balancing play provision with a need to show that children are learning can be hard work. We also have to balance the need for children to take risks with health and safety requirements, so many games and activities I remember playing are not allowed any more: conkers, marbles and climbing trees, for example. A particular challenge is making sure that staff are well trained. In education, the focus of training is often on learning and not much time is spent on play. I think good play practice relies on practitioners really understanding why play is important but there's not much training available. I've been proactive in developing my knowledge and have even started a higher degree in play. With my training and experience, I now value the process of play rather than focus on outcomes. I feel privileged when I am invited to join in children's activities and I especially look forward to free play sessions. Of course, we do some structured activities too but I try to make these playful by allowing children to take the lead. I feel more like an equal. There are often unexpected outcomes and this is exciting.

Playworkers and play development officers

Playwork is rooted in the belief that children's opportunity to play has been curtailed by modern society. Playworkers are guided by a set of principles that emphasize the freedom and spontaneity of play and as such there is a focus on open-access provision, where children can come and go as they please. Playworkers use their extensive knowledge of play to provide and enrich spaces where children can engage in activities within safe boundaries. Emphasizing children's ownership of the play, their role is often facilitative and is never directed towards a particular outcome. Positions might include work within out-of-school clubs, holiday play schemes or adventure play-grounds. Teams of playworkers might be co-ordinated by a play development officer, usually an experienced playworker who has undergone additional training.

Jo, play development officer, UK

I've been a play development officer with the local authority for five and a half years. I started with a playwork certificate but have since completed a variety of additional qualifications in community development, Forest School and youth work. I also have a master's degree in play, which extends my skills. Every day as a development officer throws up a new challenge. Variety keeps the job fresh and although I have an office base, I work at different locations to deliver training, attend meetings, run events and act as an advocate for play. All this in addition to co-ordinating the open-access play schemes and my teams of playworkers. I meet lots of different people and like to see the positive contribution that our work has on communities. People often don't recognize the importance of play, particularly risky play, for children's healthy and happy development. With the current climate of fear towards strangers, increased traffic and a perceived lack of tolerance for playing children in the community, it's particularly difficult to win people over in terms of how vital it is. You really have to believe in what you do and have a thorough knowledge of the benefits for both the children and their communities. It's not easy to change people's beliefs and sometimes it's frustrating.

Developmental and therapeutic play specialists

Specialist knowledge about the process of play and its developmental and therapeutic potential can be utilized in a range of contexts. It can be an extension to the playworker role; however, not all special-ists in developmental and therapeutic play will have this background. For example, developmental and therapeutic play is less likely to be open-access provision and activities may be developed to meet particular needs. In addition, there is increased responsibility for the individual child or group, rather than a general responsibility for the play safety boundaries of the environment (Lindon, 2001). The Irish Association for Play Therapy formalized the role of developmental and therapeutic play specialists (DATPSs) in 2008. DATPSs use play to enhance children's development and address delays, imbalance, organic difficulties or the consequences of early play deprivation. Their focus is on holistic development, promoting and expanding children's play skills to enhance cognitive, language, social, emotional and/or physical development. The work of DATPSs can have a remedial function but of importance is that it is often preventative. The practitioner may be involved with the child in the context of another professional role (e.g. teacher, playworker, social worker, speech therapist) and may utilize their play skills in the context of that role.

Kerri, developmental and therapeutic play specialist, UK

I have been working as a developmental and therapeutic play specialist in a primary school for two years. My role is to make sure children get maximum benefit and enjoyment from their experience of being at school, in particular helping them to make the most of play. The school I work in has a large multi-cultural population and I help to make sure that the play of children from all cultures is nurtured. Through play, I work with children who are finding it difficult to integrate into the school, perhaps because they are new to the area, those who need help in developing their play skills, those who have low confidence or perhaps behavioural issues. I have a dedicated playroom for one-to-one or small-group sessions and these might involve craft activities, clay, puppets or music activities. I really love my job as I get to do something I am passionate about – play. Every day is unique, rewarding and, of course, fun.

The first hospital play staff were employed in 1957 by St Bartholomew's and St Thomas' hospitals in London. Over the next two decades, the amount of staff employed in hospitals to support children's play grew significantly and, in 1972, the National Association of Hospital Play was established. While the initial focus was on providing opportunities for play while children were hospitalized, the role has grown considerably in scope and complexity over time. Hospital play specialists support children's holistic development during times of sickness and hospitalization, but also utilize focused interventions to prepare children for hospital procedures. Their observations of children's play are also used to support clinical judgements.

Hospital play specialists

Ann, hospital play specialist, UK

I trained as a hospital play specialist ten years ago, having worked for twelve years as a nursery nurse on the special care baby unit. I have been in my current post on the paediatric ward for eight years. I am one of three hospital play specialists who, with five play-leaders, make up our play team. We work closely with the nursing and medical staff and other members of the multidisciplinary team. Play has a special function in the hospital environment. It reduces anxiety, aids in assessment and diagnosis as well as speeding up recovery and rehabilitation. The children are not only ill, but are separated from their friends and familiar surroundings. Play can really make a difference, helping children to understand and cope with treatment and illness. As well as organizing daily play activities in the playroom or at the bedside, we use play as a therapeutic tool, as in the preparation of children for theatre and other hospital procedures. I am based on the busy medical ward, with ages ranging from birth to sixteen. No day is ever the same. I might start the day spending time with a toddler with food aversions – we use different tactile stimulation in the form of food or messy play. Another part of the day may be taken up with working with a child who is needle-phobic, preparing him for the necessary cannulation prior to his tonsil operation. Or I may be talking to a teenager who thinks life is not worth living after a row with her boyfriend. No one can say this job is boring or run-of-the-mill.

Play therapists

In play therapy, play is the language by which children communicate, explore and resolve issues that may be impacting on their lives. These issues might include developmental or organic problems, adjustment problems or moderate psycho-social crises. Some play therapists are also trained in psychotherapy, which allows them to consider children with more complex life histories or clinical issues. Observation and assessment skills are crucial for both the therapy process and appropriate referral. In contrast to other play professions, the focus of the work is the child's inner world, accessed in one-to-one therapy sessions, and the therapist avoids seeing the child in any other context so as not to confuse the relationship (McMahon, 2009). The profession is relatively new but is represented by professional organizations across the world. Play therapy is often a second career and training is generally restricted to those who have previous experience in working with children in some other capacity.

Mary, play therapist, UK

I have been a play therapist for eight years but have worked with children for considerably longer, having originally trained as a social worker. My days are varied, involving meetings with other professionals, assessments and work for the courts in addition to direct work with the children. In the play sessions we might use puppets, clay, sand and water. I might end up being a noisy dinosaur or a crying baby when the children involve me in their role play. The best part of my job is knowing that the children trust me to help them through bad times. I reassure them they are safe and help them to feel empowered about their future. The job is challenging on lots of levels. I often have to convince other adults about the value of play as a way for children to communicate how they are feeling.

Maria, play therapist and psychotherapist, Ireland

I have been employed as a play therapist in a service for children and adults with physical and intellectual disabilities for the past two years. I have a diploma in child play therapy and psychotherapy from the Children's Therapy Centre in Ireland. The children I work with are often at early stages of development. This means I have to balance my role in initiating play, expanding play skills as well as working on any particular issues. Their early stage of development can make it hard not to become attached. The therapeutic process can also be very slow and any benefits may not become visible as quickly as with average-ability children. The children I work with can be very sick, have extreme allergies and have very different ways of communicating their needs. This means thorough background checks and multidisciplinary teamwork are critical. I enjoy the teamwork approach – it gives me a real insight into the children's complete development and alerts me to any forthcoming issues. The majority of my work is done in a playroom. I usually have three sessions every day and these can be individuals or groups. For the remainder of the day, I might be meeting with the team, catching up on paperwork, writing reports or researching. I am in awe of my clients. Not a week goes by when I don't write down how amazing and brave they are, or how one of them has surprised me, made me laugh or surpassed some initial judgement I had of them.

Summary

- The best materials for play are often those that are the simplest.

- Space and time for play should not be unnecessarily constrained.

- Early relationships are particularly important for the development of secure attachments.

- Children's friendships develop through play as they begin to appreciate characteristics about themselves and others.

- Adults can take a variety of roles in children's play but it is important to maintain children's sense of control over the direction of the activity.

- Children's development can be supported through play by a variety of professionals.

- What challenges might adults face when interacting in play?

- What kinds of boundaries do we impose on play? Are these always necessary?

- In what ways might we increase children's sense of choice and control in play?

Give yourself some time to think

Broadhead, P., Howard, J. and Wood, E. (2010) *Play and Learning in the Early Years: From Research to Practice*. London: Sage.

Kilvington, J. and Wood, A. (2009) *Reflective Playwork: For All Who Work With Children*. London: Continuum.

McMahon, L. (2009) *The Handbook of Play Therapy and Therapeutic Play* (2nd Edition). Sussex: Routledge.

Useful reading

Useful play links

National Association of Hospital Play Staff

The professional organization for hospital play specialists: http://www.nahps.org.uk

British Association of Play Therapy

Offers training routes in play therapy: http://www.bapt.info/

PTUK

Offers training routes in play therapy: http://www.playtherapy.org.uk/

Irish Association of Play Therapy and Psychotherapy

A professional association for play therapy, therapeutic play and psychotherapy: http://www.iapt.net

International Play Association

An international non-governmental organization that aims to protect, preserve and promote the child's right to play: http://ipaworld.org/

The Association for the Study of Play

A multidisciplinary organization whose purpose is to promote the study of play: http://www.tasplay.org

TACTYC

An early years organization for anyone involved with the education and training of those who work with young children: http://www.tactyc.org.uk/

Department for Education

Responsible for education and children's services in the UK: http://www.education.gov

Play England

An organization supporting children's play in England: http://www.playengland.org.uk/

Play Scotland

An organization supporting children's play in Scotland: http://www.playscotland.org/

Play Wales

An organization supporting children's play in Wales: http://www.playwales.org.uk/

4Children

A national organization promoting play and out-of-school care facilities for all children: http://www.4children.org.uk/

National Children's Bureau

An organization dedicated to ensuring children's wellbeing: http://www.ncb.org.uk/

Children's Play Information Service

Provides information on children's play as part of the NCB's Library and Information Service: http://www.ncb.org.uk/cpis

References

Axline, V. (1989) *Play Therapy*. Edinburgh: Churchill Livingstone.

Bruner, J. S. (1960) *The Process of Education*. New York: Vintage Books.

Bruner, J. S. (1979) *On Knowing: Essays for the Left Hand.* Cambridge, MA: Harvard University Press.

Bundy, A. C. (1993) Assessment of play and leisure: delineation of the problem. *American Journal of Occupational Therapy*, 47(3), pp. 217–222.

Chappell, K., Craft, A., Burnard, P. and Cremin, T. (2008) Question-posing and question responding: the heart of possibility thinking in the early years. *Early Years: An International Journal of Research and Development*, 28(3), pp. 267–286.

Cohen, D. (2006) *The Development of Play* (3rd Edition). Oxford: Routledge.

Cooney, M. and Sha, J. (1999) Play in the day of Qiaoqiao: a Chinese perspective. *Child Study Journal*, 29, pp. 97–111.

Craft, A. (2005) *Creativity in Schools: Tensions and Dilemmas*. Oxford: Routledge.

Csikszentmihalyi, I. and Csikszentmihalyi M. (1988) *Optimal Experience: Psychological Studies of Flow in Consciousness*. New York: Cambridge University Press.

Darling, N. and Steinberg, L. (1993) Parenting style as context: an integrative model. *Psychological Bulletin*, 113(3), pp. 487–496.

David, T. and Powell, S. (2005) Play in the early years: the influence of cultural difference. In J. Moyles (ed.) *The Excellence of Play* (2nd Edition). Maidenhead: Open University Press.

Department for Children, Education, Lifelong Learning and Skills (DCELLS) (2008) *Foundation Phase in Wales*. Cardiff: Welsh Assembly Government.

Department for Children, Schools and Families (DCSF) (2008a) *Play Strategy*. Nottingham: DCSF Publications.

Department for Children, Schools and Families (DCSF) (2008b) *Statutory Framework for the Early Foundation Stage*. Nottingham: DCSF Publications.

Department for Culture, Media and Sport (2000) *Best Play*. London: National Playing Fields Association.

Department for Education and Skills (DfES) (2001) *Special Educational Needs Code of Practice*. Nottingham: HMSO.

Department for Education and Skills and Sure Start (DfES) (2002) *Birth to*

Three Matters: A Framework to Support Children in Their Earliest Years of Life. Nottingham: HMSO.

Dowling, M. (2000) *Young Children's Personal, Social and Emotional Development*. London: Sage Publications.

Erikson, E. (1963) *Childhood and Society*. New York: Norton.

Fein, G. (1981) Pretend play in childhood: an integrative review. *Child Development*, 52, pp. 1095–1118.

Garvey, C. (1991) *Play* (2nd Edition). Washington, DC: Fontana Press.

Gill, T. (2007) *No Fear: Growing up in a Risk Averse Society*. London: Calouste Gulbenkian Foundation.

Goldschmied, E. and Jackson, S. (1994) *People under Three: Young Children in Daycare*. London: Routledge.

Greenland, P. (2006) Physical development. In Bruce, T. (ed.) *Early Childhood: A Guide for Students*. London: Sage.

Groos, K. (1901) *The Play of Man*. London: Heinemann.

Haight, W. L., Wang, X., Fung, H., Williams, H. and Mintz, J. (1999) Universal, developmental, and variable aspects of young children's play: a cross-cultural comparison of pretending at home. *Child Development*, 70(6), pp. 1477–1488.

Hall, G. S. (1920) *Youth*. New York: A. Appleton.

Hines, M. and Kaufman, F. R. (1994). Androgen and the development of human sex-typical behavior: rough-and-tumble play and sex of preferred playmates in children with congenital adrenal hyperplasia (CAH). *Child Development*, 65, pp. 1042–1053.

Holland, P. (2003) *We Don't Play with Guns Here: War, Weapon and Superhero Play in the Early Years*. Buckingham: Open University Press.

Howard, J. (2002) Eliciting children's perceptions of play using the activity apperception story procedure. *Early Child Development and Care*, 172(5), pp. 489–502.

Howard, J. (2009) Play, learning and development in the early years. In T. Maynard and N. Thomas (eds) *An Introduction to Early Childhood Studies*. London: Sage.

Howard, J. (2010a) The developmental and therapeutic value of children's play: re-establishing teachers as play professionals. In J. Moyles (ed.) *The Excellence of Play* (3rd Edition). Maidenhead: Open University Press.

Howard, J. (2010b) Making the most of play in the early years: understanding and building on children's perceptions. In P. Broadhead, J. Howard and E. Wood (eds) *Play and Learning in Early Childhood: Research into Practice*. London: Sage.

Howard, J. and McInnes, K. (2010) Thinking through the challenge of a play-based curriculum: increasing playfulness via co-construction. In J. Moyles (ed.) *Thinking about Play: Developing a Reflective Approach*. Maidenhead: Open University Press.

Howard. J. and Miles, G. (2008) Incorporating empirical findings that link play and learning into a behavioural threshold and fluency theory of play. Paper presented at the BPS Psychology of Education Section Conference, Milton Keynes, November.

Hughes, B. (1999) *A Playworker's Taxomony of Play Types*. London: PLAYLINK.

Hughes, F. (2010) *Children, Play and Development* (4th Edition). London: Sage.

Hutt, C. (1976) Exploration and play in children. In J.S. Bruner, A. Jolly and K. Sylva (eds) *Play—Its Role in Development and Evolution*, New York: Basic Books.

Hyder, T. (2005) *War, Conflict and Play*. Maidenhead: Open University Press.

Hyun, E. (1998). *Making Sense of Developmentally and Culturally Appropriate Practice (DCAP) in Early Childhood Education*. New York: Peter Lang.

Isaacs, S. (1932) *The Social Development of Young Children: A Study of Beginnings*. London: Routledge and Kegan Paul.

Jarvis, P. (2006) Rough and tumble play: lessons in life. *Evolutionary Psychology*, 4, pp. 330–346.

Jennings, S. (1999) *An Introduction to Developmental Play Therapy*. London: Jessica Kingsley.

Kalliala, M. (2006) *Play Culture in a Changing World*. Maidenhead: Open University Press.

Keating, I., Fabian, H., Jordan, P., Mavers, D. and Roberts, J. (2000) 'Well, I've not done any work today. I don't know why I came to school': perceptions of play in the reception class. *Educational Studies*, 26(4), pp. 437–454.

Knight, S. (2009) *Forest Schools and Outdoor Learning in the Early Years*. London: Sage.

Krasnor, L. R. and Pepler, D. J. (1980) The study of children's play: some suggested future directions. In K. H. Rubin (ed.) *New Directions for Child Development: Children's Play* (Vol. 9). San Francisco: Jossey-Bass.

Laevers, F. (1994) *The Leuvens Involvement Scale for Young Children (LIC-YC)*. Leuven, Belgium: Centre for Experiential Education.

Lieberman, J. N. (1977) *Playfulness: Its Relationship to Imagination and Creativity*. London: Academic Press.

Lindahl, L. B. and Heimann, M. (1997) Social proximity in early mother infant interactions: implications for gender differences? *Early Development and Parenting*, 6(2), pp. 83–88.

Lindon, J. (2001) *Understanding Children's Play*. Cheltenham: Nelson Thornes.

Lindsey, E. W., Cremeens P. R. and Caldera, Y. M. (2010) Gender differences in mother–toddler and father–toddler verbal initiations and responses during caregiving and play context. *Sex Roles*, 65(5–6), pp. 399–411.

McInnes, K., Howard, J., Miles, G. and Crowley, K. (2009) Behavioural differences exhibited by children when practising a task under formal and playful conditions. *Educational and Child Psychology*, 26(2), pp. 31–39.

McMahon, L. (2009) *The Handbook of Play Therapy and Therapeutic Play* (2nd Edition). Sussex: Routledge.

Marschark, M. (1993). *Psychological Development of Deaf Children*. New York: Oxford University Press.

Maybin, J. and Woodhead, M. (2003) *Childhoods in Context*. Milton Keynes: Open University Press.

Moyles, J. (1989) *Just Playing?: Role and Status of Play in Early Childhood Education*. Buckingham: Open University Press.

National Children's Bureau (NCB) (1998) *The Charter for Children's Play*. London: Children's Play Council.

Nicholson, S. (1971) The theory of loose parts. *Landscape Architecture Quarterly*, 62(1), pp. 30–34.

O'Reilly, A. W. and Bornstein, M. H. (1993) Caregiver–child interaction in play. In M. H. Bornstein and A. W. O'Reilly (eds) *The Role of Play in the Development of Thought*. San Francisco: Jossey-Bass.

Parker, C. J. (2007) *Children's Perceptions of a Playful Environment: Contextual, Social and Environmental Differences*. Unpublished thesis, University of Glamorgan.

Parten, M. B. (1932) Social participation among preschool children. *Journal of Abnormal and Social Psychology*, 27, pp. 243–269.

Patrick, G. T. (1916) *The Psychology of Relaxation*. Boston, MA: Houghton-Mifflin.

Pellegrini, A. (1991) *Applied Child Study: A Developmental Approach*. New Jersey: Lawrence Erlbaum.

Piaget, J. (1951) *Play, Dreams and Imitation in Childhood*. London: Routledge and Kegan Paul.

Ring, K. (2010) Supporting a playful approach to drawing. In P. Broadhead, J. Howard and E. Wood (eds) *Play and Learning in the Early Years*. London: Sage Publications.

Robson, S. (1993) 'Best of all I like choosing time': talking with children about play and work. *Early Child Development and Care*, 92, pp. 37–51.

Rogoff, B. (2003) *The Cultural Nature of Human Development*. New York: Oxford University Press.

Roopnarine, J. L., Lasker, J., Sacks, M. and Stores, M. (1998) The cultural contents of children's play. In O. N. Saracho and B. Spodek (eds) *Multiple Perspectives on Play in Early Childhood Education*. New York: State University of New York Press.

Saracho, O. N. (1990) *Cognitive Style and Early Education*. New York: Gordon & Breach: Science Publishers.

Servin A, Bohlin, G. and Berlin, L. (1999) Sex differences in 1-, 3-, and

5-year-olds' toy-choice in a structured play-session. *Scandinavian Journal of Psychology*, 40, pp. 43–48.

Sheridan, M. D. (1972) The child's acquisition of codes for personal and interpersonal communication. In M. Rutter and J.A.M. Martin (eds) *The Child with Delayed Speech*. London: Spastics International.

Sheridan, M. D. (1976) *Children's Developmental Progress from Birth to Five Years*. Windsor: NFER.

Sheridan, M. (1977) *Spontaneous Play in Early Childhood: From Birth to Six Years* (1st Edition). Windsor: NFER.

Sobel, D. (2001) *Children's Special Places: Exploring the Role of Forts, Dens and Bush Houses in Middle Childhood*. Detroit, MI: Wayne State University Press.

Spencer, H. (1898) *Principles of Psychology*. New York: Appleton.

Sturrock, G. and Else, P. (1998) The playground as therapeutic space: playwork as healing [known as 'The Colorado Paper']. In G. Sturrock and P. Else (2005) *Therapeutic Playwork Reader One*. Sheffield: Ludemos.

Sturrock, G., Russell, W. and Else, P. (2004) *Towards Ludogogy, Parts I, II and III: The Art of Being and Becoming through Play*. Sheffield: Ludemos.

Sun, L. C. and Roopnarine, J. L. (1996) Mother–infant, father–infant interaction and involvement in childcare and household labour among Taiwanese families. *Infant Behaviour and Development*, 19, pp. 121–129.

Sutton-Smith, B. (1974) *How to Play with Your Children (and When Not to)*. New York: Hawthorne Press.

Sylva, K., Melhuish, E., Sammons, P., Siraj-Blatchford, I. and Taggart, B. (2004) *The Effective Provision of Pre-school Education (EPPE) Project: Findings from Pre-school to the End of Key Stage 1*. London: DfES.

Tovey, H. (2007) *Playing Outdoors: Spaces and Places, Risks and Challenge (Debating Play)*. Maidenhead: Open University Press.

Tovey, H. (2010) Playing on the edge: perceptions of risk and danger in outdoor play. In P. Broadhead, J. Howard and E. Wood (eds) *Play and Learning in the Early Years*. London: Sage Publications.

Trostle, S. L. (1988) The effects of child-centred group play sessions on social-emotional growth of three- to six-year-old bilingual Puerto Rican children. *Journal of Research in Childhood Education*, 3(2), pp. 93–106.

United Nations (1989) *Convention on the Rights of the Child*. Brussels: United Nations Assembly.

Vygotsky, L. S. (1978) *Mind in Society, the Development of Higher Mental Psychological Processes*. Cambridge, MA: Harvard University Press.

Waters, J. and Begley, S. (2007) Supporting the development of risk-taking behaviours in the early years: an exploratory study. *Education 3–13*, 35(4), pp. 365–377.

Webb, S. and Brown, F. (2003) Playwork in adversity: working with abandoned children in Romania. In F. Brown (ed.) *Playwork Theory and Practice*. Buckingham: Open University Press.

Welsh Assembly Government (2008) *Framework for Children's Learning for 3–7-year-olds in Wales*. Cardiff: Welsh Assembly.

Whitebread, D. (2010) Play, metacognition and self regulation. In P. Broadhead, J. Howard and E. Wood (eds) *Play and Learning in the Early Years*. London: Sage.

Wilson, K. and Ryan, V. (2005) *Play Therapy: A Non-directive Approach for Children and Adolescents* (2nd Edition). London: Elsevier Science.

Winnicott, D. W. (1971) *Playing and Reality*. London: Tavistock Publications.

Index